How To Ghost Hunt

Ghost Seeker Field Guides, For The New Hunters On The Block

Frank Potterstone

Ghost Seeker Disclaimer

This book contains strategies to starting your own ghost seeking team, all the methods and other ghost hunting advice that, regardless of my own results and experience's, may not produce the same results (or any results) for you. I make absolutely no guarantee, expressed or implied that by following the advice below that you will have success hunting ghosts, as there are several factors and variables that come into play regarding any ghost hunting adventure.

Primarily, results will depend on the nature of how you use this guide, the experience of the individual, and situations and elements that are beyond your control.

As with any ghost seeking adventure, you assume all risk related to investment and money based on your own discretion and at your own potential expense.

Liability Disclaimer

By reading this book, you assume all risks associated with using the advice given below, with a full understanding that you, solely, are responsible for anything that may occur as a result of putting this information into action in any way, and regardless of your interpretation of the advice.

You further agree that our team cannot be held responsible in any way for the success or failure of your ghost seeking team, as a result of the information presented in this book. It is your responsibility to conduct your own due diligence regarding the safe and successful operation of your ghost seeking team if you intend to apply any of our information in any way to your teams operations.

Terms of Use

You are given a non-transferable, "personal use" license to this book. You cannot distribute it or share it with other individuals.

Also, there are no resale rights or private label rights granted when purchasing this book. In other words, it's for your own personal use only.

How To Ghost Hunt

Ghost Seeker Field Guides, For The New Hunters On The Block

Dedicated

To my awesome and very patient wife, Teri! Whom, I love so very much. And to my little boy Frankie whose curiosity makes me laugh so much… I am so proud of him!

And finally to all the new ghost hunters out there, who share the same passion I have for the paranormal, and genuinely want to help those clients find peace and understanding for the things that go bump in the night.

Table of Contents

Ghost Seeking In the Beginning

First I must say...do you really want to go on a ghost hunt? The reason I ask, is simply because, generally a lot of people, are all talk when requesting to join a ghost hunt. But when it actually comes time to, join a hunt there nowhere to be found! It's not there fault, it's just human nature, exploring the unknown isn't everyone's cup of tea.

Are you all talk and no action? I don't think so...Otherwise you probably wouldn't of purchased the field guide your reading right now. :)

Your a Brave Soul!

Now the main focus of this book, is to get you in the right frame of mind,and well prepared before venturing out on your first legitimate ghost hunt. So the remainder of this field guide will focus on everything you need... and I mean "MUST KNOW" before heading out on your ghost hunting adventure. Following the advice below, will guarantee that in know time at all you'll be considered a Pro among your team members, and not the newbie you are right now. Again I must say please! take this advice seriously each time you go out, and I guarantee you will always have a safe and awesome ghost hunting experience, with hopefully plenty of activity to bring home to analyze.

Remember, stay safe and have a good time with your new found love for the paranormal...

And also remember even if you are a skeptic about the paranormal, please take following the protocol listed below very seriously!!!

Ghost Seeker Checklist

1.   Always and I mean always, get written permission to hunt on the premises. Some would say verbal permission is just as good, but in reality when your dealing with bumping around through someones house whether vacant or not...written permission will save your butt in more ways then one.

"Personally for myself and my team, we wont touch a property if they are not willing to sign a written permission slip to be on the property."

Better to be safe and avoid any lawsuits later on down the road, in case you end up breaking something by accident.

This little signed contract, that only takes a few seconds to sign, will save you a whole lot of headaches on down the road...trust me I've been totally there!

2. Do you have any identification on you? This should be a no brainer, but you would be surprised at how many people don't carry it on them. And if for some reason your stopped by local authorities, not having this can ruin your entire evening of ghost seeking. The main reason being, they will need this to verify that you do indeed have permission by the owner who signed the written agreement to be on the property. And I guarantee you they will check!

3. Make sure that you always hunt with somebody, never venture off on your own. You never know what dangers may be lurking about the property, and I'm not speaking of just the paranormal activity. Depending on the age of the house your investigating, there can be many physical hazards all over the place. Not to mention, if your investigating an abandoned building, there can be a different kind of danger namely gang members or homeless people that only go there at night. So it might be a good idea, if your un-sure of the surroundings to see if the local police department can do a quick sweep for you, if you have any doubts whatsoever.

"Having a cell phone with you, which I'm sure most of you are going to have is a must! After all the team comes first, you never want to jeopardize yourself or anyone else in danger!"

4. Keep all your equipment in immaculately clean shape. By having a routine, of always keeping your equipment clean and well packed away when not in use, will prevent the possibilities of registering "false positives" and destroying your findings when it comes time to reveal the activity you found to the property owner. Thus, hurting your credentials and your rep in the property owners eyes.

"This is never a good thing!"

5. Always keep in good spirits, and emit from your body as much positive energy that you can muster. Show respect for the deceased. Although, there are times when provoking does have its advantages, but for now that's not the scope of this guide, I will go over this more in a future guide. Most of the time ghosts/spirits respond and manifest themselves to you, if you don't appear threatening in anyway to them.

6. Another must, but it does take some practice, is to interview witnesses who have had an experience with the

paranormal activity. Just make sure you remain objective, try to find out if anything can be re-created by a natural means. "Debunk if you can..." but remain respectful and act in a professional manner. Remember, a lot of these folks are in some cases genuinely concerned of what's going on in their home or on their property. And gosh forbid if children are involved the level of concern rises 100 fold.

7. Do not contaminate your investigation with cigarette smoke this alone has given more false positives then anything else. "If you must smoke take it far away from where you're investigating!" And if your drinking this surely ruins all your credibility as far as if you thought you heard something. 'Nobody's going to believe you...' And besides all that...it's down right disrespectful to the property owners and the very spirits you're trying to seek. "So just don't do it!"

8. Always be sure that all your audio and video is starting on a fresh file. This practice ensures that all your recordings will have no cross contamination from recording over dirty files.

9. All team members involved in the ghost seeking should keep a detailed journal of everything they do,say and hear. That means if Bill clears his throat or happens to bump into something creating a sound, Bill needs to take note of it in his journal along with the exact time it occurred. That way, when it comes time to review the audio, video etc... Each member of the team can compare notes, and make rule out what was paranormal and what was just team noise or outside noise.

"A good habit to get into is to practice speaking to your partner, in a soft but legible speaking tone, and do so as quietly as you possibly can."

10. Under no circumstances wear cologne or perfume; reason being some spirits will let you know there around by emitting a fragrant odor. From research and even personal experience, a floral type of scent, usually represents a pleasant spirit. But, a foul pungent odor has in more cases then any represented a possible hostile spirit.

11. Is ghost hunting an expensive venture? No! It can be...but, you don't really need $25,000 worth of equipment to get some great evidence! A simple $250 to $400 digital video camera will do a great job. You can go to Radio Shack or really any electronic store and pick up a

DVR (Digital Voice Recorder), on the cheap, about $90. As far as the computer software, a basic sound en- hancement program would be fine. The only other expense you really don't want to go, to cheap with, would be your batteries "There your life blood!" These you'll want to make sure that they are specifically designed for use in your digital equipment.

12. During your recording of EVP's (Electronic Voice Phenomena) Be sure the area you decide to set the DVR down on is level, this will help rule out any vibrations from a shaky unsteady hand.

13. A couple of team members along with the client should do a quick walk-through of the house or property to be investigated. "Remember to take plenty of pictures and physically take note of areas of most paranormal ac- tivity that the property or home owner states."This is what is known as your beginning base reading."

14. Last but not least...don't come to your own conclu- sions on-site. It's always best to go over all the evidence as a team and compare notes amongst yourselves be- fore ever coming to any kinda conclusion. Keep any conclusions or personal opinions to yourself, until all

pic's, videos, and any audio has been studied fully and completely. If someone happens to ask you for your opinion on something, simply say, "We really need to try and find out what's making this happen." Never ever yell paranormal or ghost until all your investigated work has been fully completed.

The tips mentioned during this 2nd chapter, are mere guidelines to be followed to the letter, before even thinking about investigating a location. What you will learn in the upcoming chapters is everything our team does to the letter, not to mention our exact step by step process for getting the best results from all our Ghost Adventures quests.... Of course other groups of ghost seekers may or may not do things a bit different, some manage to find certain techniques work better for them then others. But the focus of this first field guide in the series of Ghost Seekers is to be as newbie friendly in the beginning, (not to overwhelm!) to get you started on bottom floor to insure that all your ghost hunts are following a well laid out process of protocols to keep you and your team members in check & safe.

Ghosts What Exactly Are They?

I'm sure most of you have seen them portrayed on TV and in the movies, they seem to be more in the mainstream now with TV shows such as: Ghost Hunters, Ghost Adventures and numerous others that are starting to jump on the TV bandwagon. And I'm sure if you haven't seen them on TV, then you have surely heard a ghost story of some type or another. But this is not TV... This is real life. Movies have a fantastic way of over doing things, to make them more unbelievable then what they really are. So whats the Truth?

Well the first question you and your team members may have before getting on with your first ghost adventure is whether or not they actually exist in the first place. the truth of the matter is this...not a single person can guarantee that ghosts exist, but on the flip side of that they can't disprove it either.

What it all boils down to, is this... even if someone scientifically proved that ghosts just don't exist, those that are true believers would still not except those findings. And the same holds true for the other side as well, if someone came to them with concrete proof that ghost do exist, they to would claim that it must be some strange elaborate hoax.

Now as for myself, and the cases I've been on, and the personal experiences I've felt, not to mention some very clear and intelligent EVP's they do indeed exist, without a shadow of a doubt. It comes down to this though...your beliefs are your beliefs... The best thing I could suggest is pay close attention to everything you see and hear, and reach every adventure with an open mind.

One thing I happen to notice a lot with newbies & even a few so called pro's, are how quick they are to label something as a ghost! There are only three types.

And they are:

Ghosts

Haunting's

& Poltergeists

And each one of these is like night & day from one another.

Ghosts or as some call "Apparitions".

Ghosts/Apparitions are the energy of someone who was
once here but now is gone. Theory tells us that some
how the person has managed to stay behind and not yet
pass over to the other side. Many call this a limbo type of
state between both worlds. The real kicker comes in, that
some may not even really know there dead. Also, when
doing an EVP session with a ghost of a person in limbo,
a lot of the times you'll get answers back to your directed
questions. Again, signs of an intelligent ghostly encounter.

Hauntings

Hauntings on the other hand, are mostly referred to as
residual hauntings, the types of experiences you'll get

from this type of haunt...would be more closer to watching a video being replayed over & over again non stop forever.

They will never acknowledge your presence, most of the time when you witness these types of haunts, certain physical conditions must be met, such as: maybe large amounts of limestone deposits, large power-lines, certain weather conditions a whole array of stuff can achieve this. Most residual haunts only seem to last for about a minute or so.

Poltergeists

Now these are some scary guys, and out of all the hauntings listed, these are the ones that strike the most fear in all clients and even seasoned Ghost hunters at times, remember the movie POLTERGIEST! Second reason, is they have the ability to affect the physical world, on a much grander level then any of the hauntings just mentioned above.

They can slam doors so hard to almost bust the hinges, heavy angry footsteps, flickering of light, like in a light show. Heavy objects moving around all over the place,. Not to mention, they can actually attack you! And most of the time they do, by pulling at your clothes or hair, scratching you & also throw things all the way across the room.

If a ghost hunter believes there's poltergeist activity going on, they know it's more or less a demon, something
that has never had a human form. Knowing this now, researchers are tending to look at this in a whole other
light.

What many now have come to find out is that, the activity
usually centers or is attached to one specific person and
his or hers own psychokinetic powers that are the cause
for the disturbances. and more times then not, they all
seem to be in adolescents that are just now reaching pu-
berty, a lot of things are going on in one's life during that
time...Emotions...Physical and Psychological stress. We
in the ghost hunting field see these as TRIGGERS for the
subconscious mind to wreak havoc with its newly found
release of psychokinetic power.

Finally by knowing the info above, you could now go into
any investigation with a totally new perspective on what
to expect and exactly what you may be dealing with on
your next encounter.

Ghost Seeking Equipment

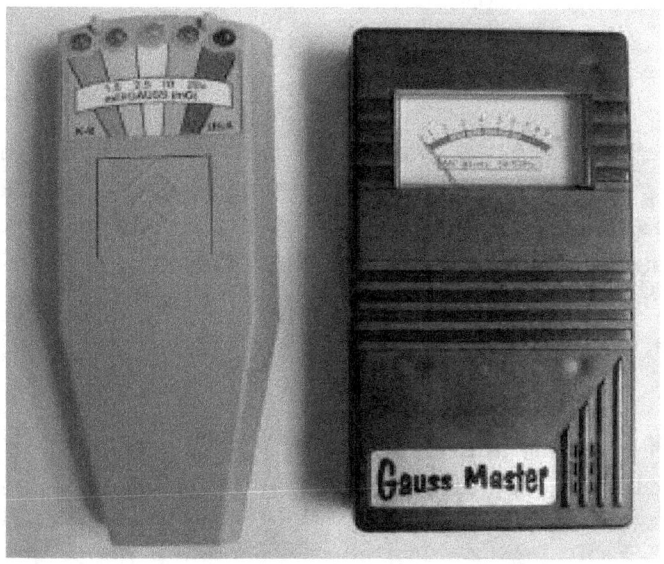

Equipment can come in quite handy on a ghost hunt don't you think? But you want to know something; you don't really need it...at least not in the beginning. Give it a try...you would be very surprised at just how, using your eyes, ears, and the rest of your body can pick up on some paranormal activity. I recommend trying just a few times; it's a great way to give your natural equipment (Your Body) a paranormal workout on your ghost seeking investigation.

Now of course, you will want the latest fancy dancy equipment eventually with you on all your investigations, to record physical proof of some kind or the other, just like you see on some of your favorite Ghost Hunting shows on TV. So let's talk about that right now.

Keeping a Journal

I see this all to often...mistakes ghost hunters make by not keeping a journal a (detailed) journal, of their ghost seeking investigation. By keeping a detailed account it insures that all your investigations, stay in sync...helping you from forgetting any important details.

Plus as an added bonus...It keeps you in check, incase you have to do any cross-referencing with any of your team members. An example would be if both of you have had an experience in the exact same place at the exact same location, you feel one thing...but your team member feels something totally different, this makes it for some strong evidence.

A Camera (Old School 35mm)

An old Pentax would work fine...just be sure you have 400 speed film on hand, or at least know where you can get some when you need it. Don't bother getting expensive Kodak film; any store brand film will do the job.

Now when you take your shots, don't use infra-red, unless you know someone that can develop it for ya, but from my experience it's a pain to find someone to develop it for you. Not to mention it's harder to find.

Black & White film works great! Just "remember!" If you are using someone to develop the film for you, be sure you tell them, that you want all the film developed, even if the film doesn't show any apparent images on it. Chances are he's not going to know what to look for, but you will!

The Age of Digital Cameras

I'd say about half of the paranormal community is still on the fence about the use of Digital cameras. One reason they seem to be against them, are they can't further examine the negatives, "because obviously Digital Cameras don't have any!" Secondly, and probably the main reason, they can easily be altered in Adobe Photoshop or really any type of imaging software out on the market today.

Now as for me, I welcome them whole heartedly, and so do the other 50 percent of ghost hunters out there. The fact is they store way more images on them...you could instantly see whatever it is you thought you caught...and if you didn't happen to catch anything, you can easily delete it right there. But the biggest point I would like to state, is that the quality of Digital cameras nowadays is remarkable, way more advanced then when they first came to market.

Your Trusty Flashlight or Torch (in some circles)

Shouldn't have to mention this, but I want to be thorough now... You will pop this out quite a few times during your investigations, just be sure you have plenty of batteries. Remember, whenever you are around a supposed haunted area the energy from the ghosts can drain them fast, "I've seen fully charged batteries, drain in mere seconds" As another option... You can get one of those (Shaker Flashlights!) "No batteries needed" You just shake the flashlight a few times and "WALA!" You have generated your own light.

A lot of ghost seekers, use headlamps because then their hands can be free for whatever instrument they are using at the time, I personally love my little Mag-light... I also bring with me a "Green Laser Pointer" it allows me to set-up a laser grid if I want too. Another nice thing about having Mag-Light is the fact that you can just loosen the back just enough where it barely takes any turning motion to turn the light on it makes for a makeshift kinda Mel-Meter of some sort. Although, it's kinda iffy, it's still pretty cool.

Keeping Time

Should be obvious, you'll need this to keep accurate records or times you mark in your journal.

Proper Clothing

Also, pretty obvious...I heard this from my mother all my life "Make sure you bring a jacket with you!" Back in the day I was trying to act all cool, going out with just a t-shirt on in freezing weather! Not bright I know, but I'm sure I wasn't the only one... Anyway, of course Mother was right! You don't need any distractions while you and your team are on investigations, and if you are not wearing the proper clothing for the weather situation, you will end up missing some possible great evidence. So always match your outerwear, with whatever the weather conditions maybe for the night.

First Aid Kit

Common sense you would think...NOT! So many people don't even think about grabbing one of these, if anything gets left behind, it always seems to be this. Obviously you are walking through some pretty dark, unfamiliar territory, someones bound to have an accident, and if you are prepared your golden.

Tape Recorder

You'll want to get a hold of a decent tape recorder that uses an external mic. Stay away from dictation type recorders most of them only have built in microphones, and they will create a ton of contaminated recordings due to the internal gears in the machine. Also never record over a prerecorded tape...always use brand new high quality tapes, and plenty of them.

Digital Recorders are nice! Especially the newer generation ones, just be sure it has an input to use an external mic, and that they record in either WAV, PCM format. I don't mess with MP3 format, too many issues.

Compass (Old School)

You may never know when your EMF meter will take a dump...this is an alternative to an EMF meter. Quite simply if the needle start moving in a crazy and erratic manner, you've just found a ghost. Other added benefit, if you don't have the latest GPS system, you can still find

your way home, "provided you know how to read a compass that is..."

EMF Detector

An EMF Detector measures electromagnetic field of an
area you're scanning. It's been stated numerous times
that ghosts can cause a fluctuation in the electromagnetic
field, letting us know they are there. Ghost presence fluc-
tuate by a reading of about 2.0 and 7.0, if you get
readings lower or even higher than this, it's a pretty good
indication that it's coming from a natural source. Also remember before doing an EMF reading, go through the
area first to get a baseline, Example...around electrical
outlets, lamps, and any other electrical device in the area, before you begin your investigative sweep.

Note: Research being done in Canada believes that once
an EMF gives off a certain fluctuation this could trigger a
physiological reaction in some part of the brain and this
can possibly alter the readings your getting. So you may
want to take this into consideration when adding this to
your kit, or at least maybe do a bit more research on these studies.

Thermometers

Every Ghost hunting kit needs to have thermometers on hand. Even though your body hitting a cold spot is quite a feeling, it's always nice to document the temperature, of the presence of a ghost, and this is a sure indication that you have someone from the other world right there with you. I personally opted in getting a infra-red non contact one...they make scanning so much easier, because they are instant in there readings.

Video Camera

A total must have! I'm not big on orbs, but when you capture them on video it's so much easier to tell if they are paranormal or if it's just bugs or dust. Still shot are always immediately throw out as dust! "Remember that!" Plus with video you get sound. It's also very important to know just how long "exactly", that the activity went on, and what caused the event to take place. Some camcorders nowadays are equipped with infra-red night vision now and some others are even full-spectrum, So not only can you see in total darkness but you have other spectrum's of light that you can see in as well. Which basically means, if there's an apparition anywhere around, the chances of you catching it are incredibly higher then it's ever been before. "Technology you gotta love it!"

Really if you were to have nothing but a camcorder I just mentioned above, you would surely catch some incredible activity on most of your ghost seeking adventures. Not to mention, that they can be set-up on tripods to watch non-stop some suspected hot areas, while you and the rest of the team, are investigating other areas.

Duct Tape, Electrical Tape

I used chalk in the past, but find myself using either duct tape or electrical tape nowadays, to mark my hot spots of supposed paranormal activity.

Walkie Talkies

Another necessity obviously, if you are part of a team you'll need to keep in communication with one another during the investigation. Headsets are another option, but for me I just click my walkie to my hip. I like my ears to be free, just to see if I happen to catch something with my own ears.

Baby Powder

I've used this a few times during my career, with some groovy results, but it's a lot messier, and I don't like that. But if you don't happen to have Motion Detectors in your budget, and your clients don't mind you spreading baby powder all over the floor, its a great alternative.

Motion Detectors

Like mentioned above...these are cleaner, but even more than that they look way more professional in the eye's of the client. How you would use them is like this...Say you have a trigger object of some sort, you would place that object down in the location that the activity seems to be taking place. Then you would set up your Motion Detector so it's covering the object and the area around it. Now if anything gets even close to the trigger object, the Motion Detectors will sound off. As far as I know there are only two types of motion detectors out there light beam barrier types and I believe passive infra-red types, there may be others, I find we tend to use the light beam ones more then anything else.

Some Quick Tips about Photos & Video before heading to the next chapter...

1.   Try to avoid like the plague, taking any digital video or snapshots during weather that's not so favorable, or where smoke and fog are visible.

2. On those cold night's, try holding your breath while taking those digital shots.

3. Always try and keep that camera steady. any movement will blur up all your shots. try keeping your elbows, locked to your side while taking the shot, it helps a great deal.

4. Kinda tough to avoid sometimes, but try to not snap shots around reflective surfaces.

5. Probably one of the most basic things to keep in mind, is make sure before you even ever get out on a hunt, that you really know your equipment inside and out. That way, when you get to your investigation, you are sure to get some great pics, audio and video.

6. Avoid any type of light sources when taking your snapshot, the glare you'll get will ruin any possible evidence you may have.

So keep in mind, whether your going on a ghost seeking venture for the first time or even if this is your 1000th time going out, the procedures and protocols I have mentioned in this field guide, should always be followed with the strictest discipline, Newbie or Pro doesn't matter.

Follow these tips and you'll be capturing some of the best paranormal activity you have ever caught, and do so in a safe manner for you and your team.

Well by now you should have a pretty decent knowledge base on some of the main equipment we use during our investigations. We use some newer stuff now like Mel-Meters, Ghost Box's, etc. Those will be discussed in detail in future volumes of Ghost Seeker. But if anything just have fun and don't worry about having to run out and by tons of expensive equipment, you really don't need that to catch some very impressive evidence of ghosts or paranormal activity. I personally know ghost seekers that go out with nothing but a flashlight and a camcorder and have a blast doing it. Others like EMF Detectors, and then there are some that think they are totally worthless. I'm sure you get the point...Everybody has there own way of doing things, that's what makes each of us unique, you decide what you want to take... and what makes you feel comfortable, and leave it at that.

Once you start gaing some ground...you may want to invest some of those donations into upgrading your equipment. The pictures below are the most widely used my Paranormal Investigators. And most can be found on Ebay, you may just luck out and get a killer deal.

EMF Meter

I.R. Camera

Laser Pen/with Grid Lens

Researching a
Ghost Adventure

I can't tell you enough, how important it is to get your facts straight, by researching a location of a potential investigation. It can totally make or break your ghost adventure.

First thing to make sure of, is activity still being reported...just because a place is said to be haunted, doesn't mean it's still being haunted. If the only reported haunt was only say, 7yrs ago, the chance of catching any paranormal activity may be slim to none.

This is exactly why researching is so darn important! This small investment of your time can reap, substantial rewards when it comes to lock-down at your location. So pull out your journal, and get that pen a moving.

The Local Library

Here you'll want to check out local newspapers that have been archived, look through the articles that pertain to the location you're researching. You can get quite a bit of Intel from this, so make note of every little tidbit you can handle, such as:

Events That Might of Happened in The Past

Possibly someone was murdered or had a horrific accident at the location your investigating. You'll want to take note of the names of all who were involved. Powerful events like this can lead to a very active location that plays over & over again.

Who were the Former Residents

A lot of paranormal activity, especially homes, prisons, castles and Hospitals are from the ghosts of those spent a great deal of time there. So, being able to track down their names can really heighten your investigation big time.

Another great Idea 'although can be pretty daunting at times' is tracking down the author who written the article on the location, getting a first hand account of the incident can prove to be very helpful. And if eyewitnesses were listed... try tracking as many of them down as well, to get there take on that day.

Another thing we do at the library is try and see if any books were written on ghost stories & folklore. Scanning through the index page of these books, can give you a quick way to see if anything has been written about the location you're investigating. And who knows, you may just find other places to investigate in the process.

Talking is Always a Good Thing.

Before even starting your investigation, arrive a couple of days before, and just talk to people in town or even the neighbors. The team and I, have received a wealth of knowledge just by doing this little step. Such as: personal encounters, local legends, and you would be surprised at some of the folks pulling out their photos to show you,'doesn't happen a lot, but does happen.'

Below are some places we keep an eye out for during per-investigation

Local Shops in the Area

Most shop owners and their employees (especially in rural areas) hear all kinds of gossip that just may be of some help.

Local Bar/Tavern

Just remember to try and get there at around the hours of 1pm to 4pm, 'you don't want to get there when everyone is well lit' the older folks, usually aren't there to get stoned drunk, they try and get there before the place goes crazy. Just be forewarned they love to talk! But this is a major benefit, because they mainly talk up a storm about the history of the place, you can find some real gems here, to help your investigation. 'Give it a Shot!'

And Of Course...Local Paranormal Groups

They seem to be springing up everywhere now, mainly due to shows like Ghost Adventures, Ghost Hunters,

Most Haunted the list continues...But, it's another added benefit, because maybe they did an investigation at your location. And if you can contact someone from there... they may just give you some valuable info right on the spot 'SCORE!'

Important Note: When Visiting Any Location...

Always be polite and respectful to those you are questioning. Some may not want to talk, and that's perfectly fine, I'm sure they have a good reason.

Never ever push yourself on them and drill them for information.

Take note of the emotional state of those your questioning. A good example would be: Suppose a little boy or girl passed only a couple of years ago, the neighbors may still be emotionally upset over this, So hitting them with a barrage of questions, in my eyes just shows a total lack of respect.

Hopefully by now, you totally understand the importance of doing proper research before going forward with your investigations.

Our Step by Step Team Procedure

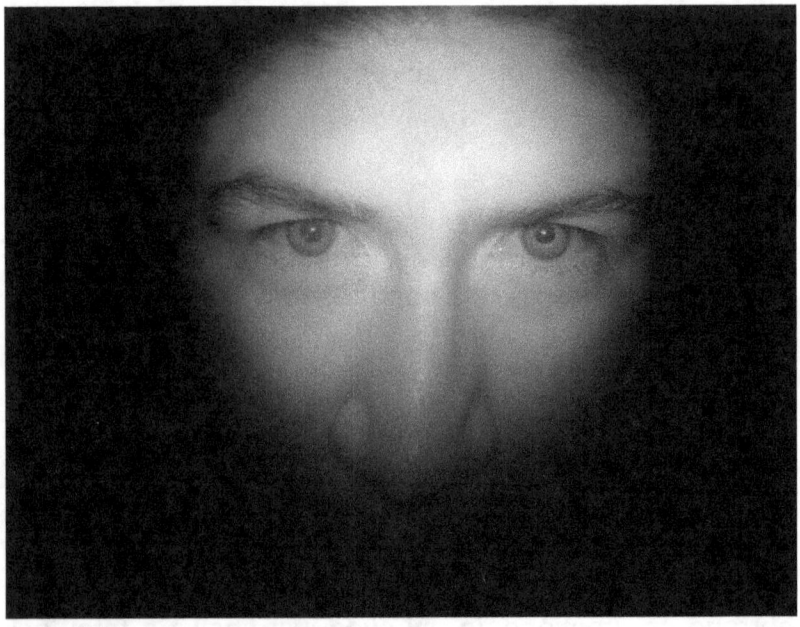

Visit the site during the day, before it gets dark

This will get you familiar with the area, and take note of any hidden dangers that may be lurking about. If you neglect doing this, you may just be asking for injuries, not to mention it's a good way to learn the layout of the location.

Huddle Up

Make sure everyone going on the investigation huddles up near the location, this is where you'll figure out who goes with whom, and what equipment your bringing into the investigation.

Pick a Team Leader

Remember, this position is not to boss everyone around, it's mainly encase someone interrupts the team Such as: police or maybe even the client themselves, picking a team leader for this is a good way to keep the investigation going.

Check All Equipment Now

Don't just make sure it works, you'll want to document, any special settings, and the exact condition of the equipment the team will be using.

A Quick Snap Shot

Upon arriving, you'll want to take a quick picture, with a digital camera, of the front of the house, building. If your at an outside location, just take some pic's of the surrounding area. The reason I say take the pic's with a digital camera, is because ghosts have a funny way of effecting the film of a standard film camera if the film has been left in the camera, about 20 minutes from getting to the location of activity. After 20 minutes have gone by, then your safe to put the film in the camera.

Start your Journal

First, you'll want to log in the Time and the Weather conditions for the night. It's really all up to you here, on how detailed you keep your journal up during the whole night of investigation. Just keep in mind, this is the way you are going to keep track and also cross reference any strange occurrences throughout the night.

Do a Quick Walk-Through

Stroll around the property for about 20 minutes or so, to get a feel of the area, but most importantly this gives ample time for the ghosts to be aware of you and get a feel for your presence. This is also a good time to break out your journal, and start taking notes on any strange feelings you may be getting from certain locations. Also this is a great time to take note of any objects that can cause false readings such as: electrical equipment, mirrors, really any reflective surfaces. This is a great time to set up any motion detectors you may have, and any other free standing equipment.

Let the Ghost Adventure Begin

Divide the team into two teammates each, 'that were mentioned above', and have them go in different directions. Have them take a few snap shots, but don't go crazy; they can also start some EVP sessions at this point.

"Remember!" Keep up with your journal...write down any strange occurrences and most importantly the times they occurred. An example would be:

- ✓ Unusual Sounds
- ✓ Meter Readings
- ✓ Any Temperature Changes
- ✓ Sightings of the Visual Kind
- ✓ Changes in how you feel emotionally
- ✓ Keeping everyone motivated, and excited about the investigation

And don't forget to give everyone on the team a chance to use each piece of equipment and the allotted time in each location. This is a great way to keep your team members from getting bored, not to mention, some people may have a better luck with certain equipment, it's a Win Win situation.

45

Time to Wrap It Up

It's so important after you have ended your investigation, to make sure all your equipment gets returned, exactly back where it's was before you started. Now, you and I know that this can be easily said but not done. Reason: Your team is wiped out! They are tired and maybe even a little loopy after the night's investigation. But, nonetheless it must be done! So it's up to you to figure out how you're going to achieve this. It's different for everybody! And this also means taking note of the condition and any settings that were set before the night comes to an end.

Leaving the Site

Pretty simple, the only thing you have to remember here is that, if the client happens to be there towards the end of the investigation; don't say a word about your findings until a thorough analysis has been done. Just leave as smoothly and as professionally as you did when you first arrived.

The Findings

The most dreaded time for most paranormal investigators... "yet the most exciting for others." This is where you find out who has what it takes, and who just plain don't... Only passionate people need apply! You must sit through hours of audio and video, and listen carefully and thoroughly during every second of audio & video. 'can anyone say RedBull!' You must also cross reference notes between different members of the team, using the info to eliminate any unusual occurrences that are explained through cross referencing, an example would be someone may have written in their journal a noise from a bedroom next door and by comparing notes come to find out another team member accidentally drop his recorder.

That's pretty much it. if you follow all the steps above and don't skip any, you have the ideal makings to be a very successful ghost hunter! 'I like Ghost Seeker!" Doesn't sound like your trying to hurt them...

Important Additional Steps whether Your Doing this For Fun or Working with a Client

Keeping Protected

A lot of ghost hunters, myself included at times, like to ask for protection with a little opening prayer when we meet at a suspected haunted location. Now I only do this if the place gives me a genuinely really creepy feeling. Also, this has nothing to do with religious beliefs, it's just an added safety measure, and only take a few seconds so in my eyes better safe than sorry.

Also don't forget to say a closing prayer as well; it's been known to stop ghosts from following you home. And like I just mentioned few seconds ago, the time that it takes to do this, is worth having the extra protection. But, doing this is totally all up to you...You make the call...

Here they are, Both Opening & Closing Prayers

Opening Prayer

Saint Michael the Archangel, Defend us in battle, be our protection against the wickedness and snares of the Devil. May God rebuke him, we humbly pray. And do thou, O Prince of the heavenly host. By the power of God, thrust into hell Satan and all evil spirits, who wander through the world for the ruin of souls. Amen

Closing Prayer

In the name of Jesus Christ, I command all human spirits to be bound to the confines of the cemetery. I command all inhuman spirits to go where Jesus Christ tells you to go, for it is He who commands you.   Amen

Top Notch Tips, For Capturing Great EVP's

This is one of the longest chapters in the book...reason being, you'll more than likely capture, more EVP's than anything else. And I really wanted to give you all the best advice on capturing, some AWESOME EVP"S right out of the gate. "Because I know for a fact! That once you get your first solid EVP... You are going to be so excited! You will never get discouraged, and you will always keep hunting for the next great EVP! So lets get started!

First off, what is a E.V.P?

It's the abbreviation, for Electronic Voice Phenomena, a few people out there, believe it's the voices of those who had passed on to the spirit world. I'm sure you have seen some of the ghost hunting shows like Ghost Adventures, Ghost Hunters, and a few others that have made ghost hunting a much more visible entity then it has ever been before.

Getting back to E.V.P's... basically in a nut shell, it captures voices from the otherside by way of Digital, Tape, Mini Disc, and a range of other devices. We still don't rightly know why we are able to catch these voices on our little devices, it still remains a mystery, but an awesome tool for our investigations, helping capture evidence for all of us, who are into parapsychology. What I like most is, you don't have to buy a whole lot of expensive equipment to get some real trophy e.v.p's. The most basic tape recorder, can net some nice 'but maybe a little rough'e.v.p's.

But, nowadays you can go to your local electronis store and pick up a dirt cheap recorder, that's actually digital that will give you some kick butt recordings! 'So why not take advantage of the latest technology if you can get it on the cheap!' not to mention its portability vs carrying around a bulky old tape recorder from the 1970's.

Another thing you going to want to look at, is its power source. You need to have some good batteries; you don't want to go cheap on these...get good grade Digital batteries. Nothing is worst than when you get to the middle of your investigation, and your batteries die,'this can really ruin your evening and your teams night as well. Also here's another little added tip before heading out for an all night E.V.P session, when buying your digital voice recorder, preferably a second generation recorder, be sure that it has a tape counter, so if an e.v.p should pop up somewhere, you'll be able to quickly get to that point of the recording much easier. Also, another tip is to have a corded microphone hooked up to your digital recorder, most digital recorders nowadays, that have built in mic's also have a jack to hook up an optional corded microphone.

This is always much better then built in mic's and also cut's down the static or any other interference that a built in microphone may give, due to the internal parts of the recorder itself.

And you know, as well as anybody else anything that you can do during your investigation, to minimize any chance of cross contamination, is going to make your life much easier, not to mention saving you headaches during your analysis after you pack up for the night.

keep to your protocol never forget this. Your equipment is only as good to you...as you are as good to it... So be sure that you treat your equipment as if they were your kids, because it's that very equipment, that you may just get that prize winning one of a kind proof that will put your name in the history books.'you may never know.'

Your First Recording

Now whether you're a religious person or not, it's always a good idea to start your sessions off with a little opening prayer and finally a closing prayer at the end. The reason behind this is just a saftey measure, and not everybody does it...But, to me it's better to be safe then sorry, I don't need any little vistors following me home. :) But, feel free to use your own judgment.

If you need to get a hold of opening & closing prayers, just do a quick search in google, you'll find a whole bunch of them... That way you can pick and choose which ones you might want to use for all your E.V.P sessions.

Now getting, on with your first recording, do a quick two minute test with your digital recorder. Go ahead and set the volume to its highest setting, and then start recording.

Quick Note: If your model of recorder has one of those voice activated switches, turn it off there useless in my opinion; you'll always want to manually hit the record button, that's the only way to do it!

Ok back to where we were...What you want to listen for is machine noise or other interference. If you get to much interference coming in, you'll want to get another recorder. So a good bit of advice would be, to try and do this at the place of purchase, so you can swap it out if you need to.

So once you have a device with minimal noise interference, go ahead and set the recorder down on a nice flat non metallic surface, if you happen to be by a window or door, heater, vents, air conditioning units, move it to another area, sound travels right through windows,and I'm sure you can guess the reasoning behind getting away from the other mentioned items. And you don't want to contaminate your recordings before you even get started.

53

That also means keeping your recorder away from power lines as well; they can wreak havoc with your digital recorder.

Once you have found a place to set down your recorder, or maybe perhaps you find it easier just to hold on to it instead, either way... you'll want to refer to the basic questions mentioned in Vol 1, but I'll just go ahead and mention a few of them here again so you don't have to go through the trouble.

Anyone here, that would like to come forward and speak with us?

Are you a female or maybe even a male?

Tell me what is your name?

What makes these questions go from basic to advanced, is really all about the tone you use in your voice. If you have ever watched Ghost Hunters the TV series, you may have noticed an episode where they had a celebrity "Meatloaf" now he wasn't a seasoned ghost hunter, just starting to get into the field. But, he was awesome! When he asked questions he really put a lot of feeling and emotion into communicating with the other side. That's why when it came time for the reveal, they had caught some killer E.V.P's.

You have to be able to communicate to the other side as if you know that they are there without a shadow of a doubt, just as if you were talking to a friend of yours or maybe even a family member, stranger whatever the case may be. It's during that time, when you start to feel comfortable with the way that you are communicating, is when you'll catch some very clean strong E.V.P's.

Just make sure that while your taking these basic questions and making them yours, that you allow a good little pause between questions, to give the other side a chance to actually answer them.

If you happen to be doing an E.V.P session in the great outdoors, be sure to always pick a day where the weather is nice and calm, without the wind. Also, practice whenever you get the chance inside & outside, recording yourself walking around various areas, sound has a way of traveling further then you may think.

This reminds me, of one very important step that you must always...and I mean always...Remember! During your sessions, you are bound to cough, bump into things, trip at times; these of cource are all sounds that will be caught on your handheld digital recorder. Thus, being sure that you always tag any sounds such as clearing your throat, and what I mentioned above from you or any team member. Otherwise, you are going to be driven crazy during the analysis. "Fair Warning"

So be sure if you have a team going out with you on these sessions, that they are well aware that they must and always should tag any physical noises they make while exploring through the supposed haunted location.

E.V.P Hot Spots

Truthfully, anywhere can be an E.V.P hot spot your own house or back yard. You have to adjust your thinking, in a broader dynamic. Every square inch of this planet, can and does have some sorta activity, some of course greater then others, but the fact remains... This planet is quite old, and many, many generations have lived all over the surface of this planet.

Was your home, where it is now, let's say about 100yrs ago or so? Maybe? How about 300yrs ago?

You kinda of get what I'm saying now? We live in a world of paranormal activity, it's everywhere.

But, again you might as well try the tried and true first. What I would suggest is that you locate some of the known haunted places in your area first. And because the internet is such a god send to all of us, it makes finding these places very easy. I betcha, even your own neighbors who you may or may not associate with much, might even have some stories to tell you themselves, and might even let you do an E.V.P session in there own home.

Just be sure as I mentioned in vol 1, that if they do agree to have your team to a session, that you get it in writing!

I would even go as far... 'all depending on how far you want to take this...' to get yourself and your team insured bonded, nothing spells trust as much as the word BONDED! This insures you, in case you break anything, that you can replace it. Plus, this builds trust for your clients. They want to feel safe and secure in there decision to let you in on there property, and being insured will get you more clients for sure.

Other locations to check out, could be your local cemeteries, if you're not to freaked out by that. Just be sure to have respect for the loved ones who have passed on. Try not to walk on any graves, nothing shows dis-respect more then when somebody walks on ones grave. My trip to Chapel Hill cemetery here in Colorado, netted me about 15 E.V.Ps back in 2009, some were so clear, you would swear a buddy of mine was with me...but, nobody was with me on that haunted night.

Also, believe it or not, some know UFO sighting places tend to yield some very decent E.V.P's, something to do with the natural earth energies, so if you know of any of these places, they would be much better to check out, then let's say your house or maybe back yard.

Here are some more Example Questions To Ask

1. Anyone one here, that would like to come forward and speak with us?

2. Are you a female or maybe even a male?

3. Tell me what is your name?

4. Were you married,or are you all alone?

5. Can you make some noise, anything to let us know that you are here?

6. If we snap a picture will we see you?

7. Do you not want us here?

8. Are you even aware that you have died?

9. Do you have any idea what year it is right now?

10. Why do you like it here so much?

11. Do you want to be free of this place?

12. How did you die,were you killed?

13. Is there someone alive that you would like us to give a message to?

Analyzing All Your Data

For some this is the best part, of the investigation, for others not so much... Some of your team members may try and skip out on this one, feeding you one excuse after another. That's OK, your passionate enough about it, to do it all by yourself if you have to.

Yes it's grueling, at times' well most of the time, but it well worth it, when you finally catch something, the feeling you can't really even put into words!' Oh and by the way if your team decides to skip out on ya during this part of the investigation, be sure to not show them the E.V.P's for a full week or so...Who knows next time around you may just have some volunteers help you out :) 'Now that's just, how I handle it, you don't have to do that' 'that's just how I roll :)'

OK now drifting back to what you need to do first:

You have gathered up every bit of your E.V.P sessions, in front of you at the table. Now for the daunting but "exciting!" analysis of each and every tape. You're going to have to go through each and every question you had asked, and listen to every un-natural sound that your device recorded.

Don't expect immediately to of hit and E.V.P from the other side, 'although sometimes you may get lucky right off the bat.' Most of the time though you're in for a long night, and unfortunately sometimes nothing surfaces at all. This is what tests your passion for this field, if you get absolutely no E.V.Ps and your still wanting to go to your next session, you truly have the makings of an excellent,passionate Ghost Hunter. You have to remember this too, the quality of you evidence also depends on the quality & sensitiveness of digital recording device. But, don't forget! You can enhance the audio using a PC nowadays... So if you are having trouble listening to the recorder by itself, hook it up to a PC so you can hear a spectral analysis and isolate and amplify the recorded pauses , you just may get a most welcomed surprise!

But like I talked about earlier, you really don't need very high tech equipment to capture great E.V.Ps. 'If you can afford it great, more power to ya, but it's not necessary.'

I have old E.V.Ps, that are on a Dictaphone 'Now that's old!'

And some of them are even clearer then the ones I catught with a digital recorder. And I'm sure I have a few dozen or so that I caught using just an old school cassette tape recorder. The point is you can easily get caught-up in the high tech world of must have, but don't let that stop you from recording and going through your first analysis of your E.V.P session.

If you let money get in the way you'll never get going on retrieving possible golden E.V.Ps.

Bonus Section

Now, although I swear by my Digital recorder, I must admit, I still find myself relying on my old tape analog recorder, and there's a good reason for it, as you'll see below. So that being said here's my best tips to acquiring the best E.V.Ps you'll ever get.

First off if you have an actual taped recording of your E.V.P, it will be highly regarded as an authentic recording. Now, I'm not saying digital is bad; it just that EMF energy from spirits can sometimes cause a bit of interference with digital recorders, creating a noise that can sometimes cover what an entity might be trying to say.

Believe it or not, you can sometimes trick a ghost. By saying something like 'So is this place, always this dark?' basically what you're doing is instead of coming right out and saying 'Is there anyone here?' You are already establishing to them that you already know that they are there. I can't even begin to count how many time this has worked for me in the past, and I have gotten some great responses. Be sure to give it a try for yourself.

Don't be afraid to ask the Ghost to speak up clearly! Show them the microphone, and explain why they must speak up. Tell them that you won't be able to hear them if they, can't speak clearly into the microphone.

This has always worked with my kids, so I figured why not with the spirits. I'd try and make a deal with them. I'd say something like this, 'hey if you will answer this question, I promise I will bring you what ever it is that you want if I'm able to retrieve it readily at hand. Just make sure you don't promise them something you can't deliver. 'You don't want to be known as a man or a woman, not of his or her word, in the spirit world!'

Try not to use if any noise filtering/reduction during recording. Leaving the hiss in is totally fine, it actually helps the recordings from sounding metallic or plastic like. I tell ya far to many people use this effect. Instead of messing with noise reduction, try even a subtle hiss reduction instead, and then try compressing the audio a bit. Then you will be able to pick up, on things that are much quieter much more impressively while turning up the volume. Much better than taking it away with noise reduction.

Important!!!

1. Never whisper, speak in a very soft and clear voice.

2. Note by ear any sound heard.

3. This should be obvious, but sometimes not so much...make   sure jewelry or change from your pockets are left somewhere other then your person, like in a bag in your vehicle.

4. We covered this already, but I'll say it again...carry plenty of batteries designed for digital audio and video.

5. Always take note of the date, time, and your location that you are doing your recording.

6. Try and keep all your EVP sessions short. Make it much, much easier to review later.

7. Keep the questions simple, and allow at least 25 seconds for an answer to come through, before asking another question.

These are only a few tips for catching some real nice EVP's. Of course, when speaking to spirits, you'll want to ask these questions with a little bit more of your persona, as if you really were talking to a friend. Using a very positive emotional energy, friendly spirits will feel more comfortable to communicate with you. Also, try to team up with a male and female and take turns asking questions. Just like in real life, some spirits may feel more comfortable communicating with one sex instead of the other.

Never get angry and start yelling at a spirit, always remember even if the spirit is friendly by nature, this can surely upset him or her very quickly, and can possibly, though rarely cause you or one of your team members harm. That's why I find asking simple questions instead of long drawn out questions to work the best. And I also usually keep it at about 4 questions, before I decide to move on. Trust me, If they want to say something they'll surely let you know.

Equipment Tips

Try an pick up a fairly inexpensive but decent external microphone, much better than using the mic that comes with the recorder.

Headphones, again they don't have to be expensive, but when your listening to E.V.Ps, it's always better to do so using headphone that isolate the sounds theater like into your ear, providing you with a much better chance of catching that all and sometimes illusive E.V.P.

Starting Your Own Ghost Seeker Team

Step 1: First thing you are going to need to figure out... Is exactly what type of paranormal investigators you'll want to be? Paranormal is a wide field. Do you want to hunt ghosts, UFO's, Aliens, Cryptozoology.These are all considered part of the paranormal. So take some time and focus on what part really interests you..."Obviously you bought this book, so I'm figuring Ghost Hunting would be your answer!" Nonetheless, I just wanted to put it out there to show there are many aspects to the paranormal world.

Step 2: Finding people who share the same interests into the paranormal to join your team, "Is definitely the way to go!" Friends are always the best choice. The more cases you do together that are successful, you'll start noticing a few others wanting to join up with your little band of brothers.

Now, if for some reason or the other, you have no friends that are interested in the Paranormal... Don't dispair! You'll find multitudes of paranormal friends who you can target to your exact city or state just by browsing trough some of the well known social sites such as: Facebook, Twitter, Linkedin, Myspace "I think that's still around...not sure." Anyway, "You get the point!" All you really have to do is post that you are looking for some paranormal fans to join your team here in "Whatever state you are living in at the time." And you should get quite a few replys back to ya! So there you have it... that's how easy it is to find people who share your same interest.

Step 3: Choosing a team name. What to remember here is in general...team name are chosen by the area that they happen to be living in at the time. Example would be: Rocky Mountain Paranormal Society. The only problem with this strategy is if someone who is in need of your help lives in a totally different county they may be a little reluctant in contacting you. "Not always the case, but it does happen."

Then there's another way to go about it, that doesen't tie one down to just a regional area. Make it Non-regional! Example: High-Tech Paranormal, by choosing a name

68

like that, you can basically go anywhere you wanted to around the world.

Step 4: Considering Roles of Each Team Member. This can be as deverse as you want it to be..." I wouldn't get to crazy with this though."

Who do you want to asign as your Equipment Tech? (The one who has the most experience with electronics)

Who do you want as your investigators? (The one's that follow through with each and every lead)

The all important Skeptic. (The person who questions everthing, and debunks what he can) "Although, I personally believe, each team member should do this!"

And finally...You're Case Manager? (This person should be the definition of the Most Friendliest, Likable person in the world that has an amazing ability to open up many dooors! She or He will be responsable for taking all the calls from clients. There are numerous historical places that will bring you in for an investigation, but don't count on them contacting you anytime soon. It will be up to your Case Manager to hunt these places down and do some schmoozing to get you in.)

69

Now this next part I leave soley up to you. It involves the use of pyhcic's... Now, I personally like to keep my team in the realm of being tech oriented. But, I have from time to time used a friend who just so happens to be a Sensitive, and have had some great results with her.

It's always good to have these people on standby. Reason being some clients, may believe that the accounts going on in their homes are of a Occult nature.

The Psychic. (What they like to be called, nowadays is Sensitives. The word Pychic has been tarnished by charlatans.)

A word of Warning when using a pychic though... Other paranormal groups "If word gets out!" May try and discredit you by calling you "Devil Worshippers!" I know stupid huh...but sadly it does happen. The funny thing is some of the other teams use them too, but they just hide them better. Personally, I do whatever it takes to make the client feel relaxed and comforted. So if taliking to a pychic makes them feel better so be it, in my book. What it all really boils down to is this...not every client you meet will share the same religion or beliefs, so you have to do whatever you need to do, to make them feel relaxed.

Step 5: Setting Up Team Meetings.

(Can't stress enough, on how important this is...whether you do it by-weekly or weekly, monthly, quarterly it's really up to you to decide. A lot can be accomplished by having a deciplined meeting. The team feels a sense of structure; they feel that they are actually part of a professional outfit. Not to mention any new ideas, concerns can all be addressed during these team meetings. And also these meeting are a great platform for lecturers to speak to the team as a whole. " A great learning experience!"

Step 6: Equipment.

Not a whole lot is needed when first starting out. "For one thing the funds just won't be there when first starting out." So for this quick (how to)...we'll assume your on a very tight shoestring budget.

First thing you'll need to find out is, what you do happen to have as far as equipment is concerned. Go to all your team members, and have them take a quick inventory of what they can add to the team.

Here's a standard equipment list:

- Flash lights

- Pens and Note Pads

- 2 way Walkie Talkies

- Tape recorders or Digital recorders

- 35mm film cameras or Digital cameras

- Tape or Digital Camcorders

- (you may or may not find these in your garage or basement, but they are nice to have.) IR Thermometers, EMF meter.

-Optional but very useful.

An external Microphone! Reason being, most tape recorders that have built in mics, tend to pick-up all the sounds of the mechanics running the recorder "Metalic sounds". And can be quite frustrating!

The few items listed, should be relatively easy to find around your house. Most people have flash lights along with pen and paper. Also I'm sure most of you have digital cameras at the ready. If you have both digital and 35mm film cameras that's just an added bonus. "I've caught some real nice images on 35mm! And as far as evidence is concerned it's hard to beat 35mm film.

Everyone and their mother know's that EVP's are really hot right now! If you cant find a recorder lying around, just head on down to Wal-Mart or Radio Shack. You can pick up a real decent recorder there, for almost pennies. Wal-Mart carries one digital recorder by Sony that can plug into your computor to save audio files and also comes with earbuds. And while you're at Wal-Mart you might as well pick-up a IR thermometer they are relatively cheap as well. And to find a cheap EMF Meter just surf Ebay. You'll find some great deals on some decent EMF Meters there.

Not to bad "HUH!" You'll be surrised at how much you and your Team (Who are also youre friends) can come up with.

Step 7: Now for the fun part designing your logo and banner, and also creating a website where all your potencial clients can contact you and interact with your site. It's really not that hard, and can actually be quite fun. I try to stay away from a ton of flashy stuff, tends to be a hassle for the users to navigate through. They just want to see some evdence that you and your team have caught. Maybe even read through some of the cases you and your team were involved with. Maybe some reviews from other clients about your services. And most im-portantly, have a way in which they can get a hold of you.

You'll be tempted, to add all types of stuff to your site such as: Terminology, Tips etc. but you really don't need to do that! The only people that would get into all that are Members of your team or teams getting ready to start their own group. Clients can really care less about all that. And besides too much information, gives you a whole other problem such as: Page loads way to slow! And you also don't want to give Information Overload to any potencial clients! So just keep it simple, and it will be great! Another important thing to remember is, to constantly check your email...you don't want to leave your clients hanging!

There are a number of free services to start out at like: Blogspot.com, wordpress.com, Weebly.com, Googlepages.com etc. (All these sites allow you to set-up a nice site for your clients to visit. Once you start coming into some money "Through donations, or your other job..." You can get a nice website set-up at Hostgator.com go with the (Baby Package) it allows you unlimited domains (Which are website) for a low cost of $7.00 a month. You still have to register a name for each site you build... about $8.00 per year. But, it's still a great deal! And looks a lot more professional when you have a yourname.com vs yourname.weebly.com

Also there are some free services available out there for voicemail through the internet, which makes it real easy for clients to get a hold of you.How it works they leave a message, and you get an Email as soon as it's been rec-orded. "Very Cool!"

Designing your Logo

You can do this youself or hire someone through a site such as Fiverr.com just type into there search box "Logo Design" and quite a few designers will pop-up! The best thing about fiverr is everything costs just $5.00 and the quality of work some of them do for $5.00 is really amaz-ing. But, use common sense here and only hire the ones who have raving reviews! Another option would be doing

74

it yourself, through free opensource programs such as: Gimp.com, Paint.net etc... You can find many tutorials online at Youtube.com covering both these programs. "And it's actually really fun to do for yourself!" But first, whether you go the paid route or free route... you'll need to come up wth a design in the first place. And I believe every member of your team should have a vote and some design input into the Logo that best represents you and the team. A good thing to bring up at the meetings! "So let the creativity begin!" Some paranormal teams out there, get really into incorporating the occult symbols in their logo. Which some Iv'e seen look really nice. And then there are some Iv'e seen that are as plain Jane as they come, and just have colored boxes to the left of their name. "I like the other methodmuch better!"

Step 8: Finding Clients

This may seem like a daunting task in the beginning, but it really isn't as tough as you might think. "Especially, if your Case Manager, can sell herself like no other!" The fact is though, there are so many people out there who may need your help, you will be shocked at just how many, once you start to make your move in this field. But, to get you started in the beginning try: Utilizing the web for contacting clients that may need your help. Visit some of the message boards that many towns,counties and states have set-up on their websites. Quite often you can sign-up for these websites...create a username "Something that's related to your Paranormal Team!" Once your all signed up post messages on the Community Board stating, your services. Leave away for them to Private Message (PM) you...many may not nessesarily what to write about their experiences, where everyone can see! So, keeping it private works best for them, I promise you

75

keep up with this technique, future clients will come to you!

Flier's "What can I say about them...as old and true as time itself!" "Don't smirk!!! They still very much work!" We've got quite a few clients this way our selves... You can also, place small ads in your local papers...nowadays you can get this done so cheap it's crazy. Largely, due to the fact that most Newspaper places are experiencing some major shortages in profits, also due to the way technology has just skyrocketed the past few years. " I still support my Newspaper Agency the Denver Post! Im sentimental...I love the smell and feel of real paper be-tween my fingers!" "Ok enough of that... Sorry! Lets move on" Another great way to utilize your Team Meetings to the fullest! Pass around a donation bin or just have one set up at your meetings. The funds it recieves can go right back into the Team by paying for ad space, updated equipment, yhe list gos on! The most important thing to get from all this is "GET THE WORD OUT!!!"

Step 9: Procedure Set-Up (During Investigation)

Professional conduct examples: If you're a smoker (De-fine smoke breaks and an area away from the investigation area.) Setting up an area just for breaks such as Drinks and food is a great idea! If you happen to be investigating at a residence...try and move your break area to your vehicle.

A simple code of conduct! (Feel free to edit this list to your liking, nothing is ever set in stone!)

1. Take your smoke breaks, once every hour or so for about 10 minutes and only at the designated break area, never during an actual investigation being conducted.

2. Leave all food and drinks at the designated break area.

3. All members must wear their black shirt wit company logo and blue jeans during the investigation.

4. ANd above all else...each and every member must watch their language around clients. Violation of this simple task of following any of these codes will result in the immediate dismiss of any said member from (your team name here.)

Step 10: Paperwork and Case Reports.

One of the very first things you should do! Is create a release form...

"Luckily you bought this book! I will have a sample of one in the back of this book along with other, much needed forms!"

These forms are to be filled out for each client whose home or dwelling you and the team are planning on investigating...they must be signed by the client! If you are creating these forms on your own, just be sure they sound professional and that it will release the team and yourself of any legal action that may take place in the strange event that something happens at the clients home or dwelling, building or place of business. I know all this may seem extreme, but trust me...in the long run you'll be glad you did! Most clients have absolutely no prolem whatsoever in signing this document. Mainly we have these forms to protect us, from having the client come back at a leter date and accuse us of stealing something that may actually be something they misplaced, and just forgot about. "It Happens!" So an once of prevention will save you and your team a bunch of headaches!"

Other paperwork to consider having is: Designed for the members of yourself and the team. Is an Emergency Contact Form "You can find dozens of these online...but, they are pretty simple to draw up yourself." All it needs to include is the Name of each member of the team, phone number, street address, and at the minnimum 2 people to contact in case of an emergency. And be sure you ask for their number as well! This should be a requirement no matter what!

Case reports are fairly simple as well. "Again, I have given you a sample case report at the back of this book YAY! for you! Although it's created for outside investigations, you can just adapt it to apply for inside investigations with no problem whatsoever!" Anyway, the structure to a nice Case Report is as follows: It must have all members personal experiences listed. A well typed out layout of all physical and pychic evidence were found. A place for the Date and Time. These should all be able to print out or be able to burn to a CD, to give to your clients so they can review it as well. "IMPORTANT NOTE!" Be sure to always make three copies! One for your team, one for the client, and one to keep as a back-up!"

Step 11: Constantly feed your mind!

There's a whole wealth of knowledge out there thanks to technology. "In the resource section of this book, I list quite a few places online that will keep you stimulated! Just keep in mind, like anything else online there's also a bunch of whooey too. So use your inner self, in guiding you the right way! If it doesen't sound right to you then it may not be! Research and cross check everything, never take anything as Gospel, right off the bat!"

Terminology is another thing you'll need to get real familiar with..."Don't forget to go through that section of the book!" The terminology covered will be on Equipment, and theories. This will help aid you in not only talking to other paranormal investigators, but most importantly to your clients who have many questions to ask you. You will be able to give them honest intellegent answers.

Other places to research are local book stores, and Libraries. "Just be careful, along with good knowledge...there are also alot of crazy stupid theories out there as well.

Something also to consider "and I believe I mentioned this a bit earlier on in the book" Be real weary of Team member you brought onto the team without really knowing who they are. That's why I always suggest working with friends at first "at least in the beginning stages of development." The problem with bringing on strangers you really don't know yet, they could be wanted by the police "Don't laugh it's happened to us at one time!" They may just have a police record. I'm all about second chances, but the fact is many clients may not take to kindly to you letting in someone that may or may not steal from them. "Play it safe and do a good screening!"

A good practice to get into is not to run to your client every 5 minutes to disclose and evedence you or may not have caught. ALways wait until you have gone over everything and have an actual case report to present them. Another thing you want to let just your team members know is to tell them to write down every experience they encounter and not to share it with everyone else. At the end of the investigation will be a good time to share all the personal and physical experiences.

Don't be afraid to make friends with other paranormal groups. It's an awesome way to continue your growth as an investigator. Not to mention, share resources, members, equipment, and even in some cases share actual cases themselves. This work great if some clients contact you, but they are a bit out of your area. And the same works the other way around. "It's a WIn Win situation!"

Probably my biggest pet peeve of everything to do with the Paranormal Investigators! The ones who charge a client for their services, nothing erks me more!!! I have found, that in most cases that happy client's just naturally feel a need to donate to your cause. "Which I'm totally fine with!" The point is, you genuinly help a client out with no intentions of money ever changing hands. You had done the job because you as a team actually care about the things that go bump in the night. If you chose to be an investigator just because you want Fame and fortune your getting into the wrong field for that! But, that's not to say you won't be well rewarded for all your hard work and dedication! You will of helped many people who are afraid of what might be going on in their world, come to some sort of peace! "All because you care about what you do...and want to honestly help these people!" That is what it really all about! "Ok I'm off my silly Soap Box!"

Please keep your manners in check around clients! A lot of people out there believe that this is only being person-able "OK!" Nonetheless, show respect and you'll get respect right back at ya! That's my feeling about being Personable!

There can be a lot of nut jobs in this field! Watch your backs! A lot of them love the paranormal field, remember to always question everything.

Just like you have trouble makers in real life, you are bound to run into some during your paranormal career. These are the guys who want to be the world's greatest paranormal team, and will stop at nothing to get there. These are the people I kinda mentioned earlier, the one's who get into it strickly for the chance that they may become famous and have huge Television deals. "I'm here to tell ya, not that it can't happen...but, you would have more of a chance in winning the lottery "Sorry but, it's a very competeive field!" "Good Luck though if that's your goal!" All I can say as I finish writing this chapter is...Just be yourself and let your reputaion litterally speak for itself.

Ghost Seeker Terminology

Akashic Records: Originally a Hindu concept of a vast, and ever increasing, psychic repository of every thought and emotion - human or otherwise - which has ever been, and into which some individuals seem able to tap.

Agent: A living person at the site of a haunting. Some human agents act only as witnesses to paranormal events while others are believed to be the method by which the hauntings occur. Some agents may cause phenomena to increase, while others may be the entire source of the activity. How this works is as yet unexplained.

Amulet: A symbol with magical significance, which is worn as a pendant or ring.

Angel: "Messenger of God," a celestial being, benevolent in nature and if visible, appearing in human form, and possessing miraculous abilities such as teleportation, healing powers and knowledge of future events. There have been accounts of angels aiding people in times of crisis throughout the ages, albeit with no real consistency to their 'modus operandi.'

Anomaly: An occurrence or condition removed from ordinarily understood experience.

Apparition: The projection or manifestation of a quasi-physical entity.

Apport: A physical object that can materialize and appear at will and can include coins, watches, jewelry and even food. They are often connected to spirits who interact with the living as the spirits cause items to appear and disappear in an effort to make themselves known.

Astral Travel: Belief or theory that a person's spiritual awareness can temporarily detach itself from the physical body, remaining connected by what is called the "silver cord," and experience things in other locations, time frames or dimensional planes. Some refer to this as "Astral Projection" or "Mind Projection."

Aura-world: A reflection of our own sphere of existence, composed of the electromagnetic emanations of physical matter, and probably influenced by thought and emotion. It is another dimensional plane proceeding from one in which we exist.

Automatic Writing: A method used by spirit mediums to obtain information from the next world. It is believed that spirits take control of the medium and cause them to write unconscious information on paper.

Banshee: A death omen or spirit that attaches itself to certain families.

Banishing: Formal, ceremonial, procedure affected to cast an invisible presence or influence out from an area. This term can refer either to a spiritual cleansing, or the closing of a magical rite, when the invoked powers are dismissed.

Bogey: A spirit that is particularly antagonistic toward humans, traveling alone or in groups to cause trouble.

Channeling: A modern method of spirit communication in which the spirits pass information directly to the medium, who then repeats the information for the listener.

Clairaudience: The experience of receiving paranormal information through auditory impressions, voices and whispers. Many psychics are said to receive information from the spirit world in this manner. It can also be used to describe voices and whispers heard in haunted locations.

Cleansing (Psychic): A less ritualized form of exorcism, where-in a dwelling or site is purified and malevolent influences are banished through prayers, spoken as the petitioner moves through the area.

Collective Apparition: A type of ghost sighting that occurs when one or more people see the same apparition.

Control: A spirit who acts as a medium's connection with the next world, also referred to as a "spirit guide".

Construct, Psychic: It has been theorized, and experimentation has been conducted to support this premise, that through directed psychic energies a responsive spirit-like entity can be created, continuing for a time to exist independently.

Crypto-zoology: The branch of paranormal research which deals with the exploration of legendary creatures such as Bigfoot, lake and sea monsters,

Thunderbirds, etc. It should be noted that the Giant Squid (the "Kraken"), orangutans (the "Red Men of the Forest"), Komodo Dragons and gigantic Nepalese elephants all were formerly included in the roster of fabled creatures!

Crystal Skulls: Five human skull models, exquisitely crafted in antiquity from solid quartz crystal, have been found in various locations throughout Latin America, the best known of these being the 'Mitchell-Hedges Skull,' discovered in 1924 in the Balese Jungle of Labuton by Anna Mitchell-Hedges while on an expedition with her father, and still in her possession in Canada. The others are kept in collections in Guatemala, Texas, the Smithsonian and the British Museum. Mayan legend tells that eight more crystal skulls remain, and that by the time all thirteen are united, mankind will have learned how to extract and decipher the vital information, history and revelations, which they contain.

Demon: Hostile and resentful entity, supposedly of non-human origin, which some believe to be "fallen (from grace) angels."

Dematerialization: The sudden disappearance of a person or spirit in full view of witnesses.

Discarnate: A word used to describe a spirit or specter...literally means "without flesh".

Doppelganger: Meaning "double image", it is thought to be an exact spirit double of a living person. They are considered to be very negative in nature.

Earthbound: Refers to a ghost or spirit that is unable to cross over at the time of death. Many spirits make the decision to remain behind by choice while others are too confused or frightened because of a sudden death or suicide to make the crossing.

Ectoplasm: An organic material that was supposedly exuded by physical mediums during séances as a way of proving contact with the spirit world. It would often take certain shapes. The substance was supposed to appear from just about any orifice of the medium's body. In more recent times, many researchers believe the substance had a natural form, created by fraudulent mediums during the Spiritualist era.

Electronic Voice Phenomena (EVP): Voices and sounds that are alleged to be from the dead and that are captured by electronic mediums on tape (digital recorders, tape recorders, etc.). Disembodied "voices" and sounds imprinted on audio recording devices.

Elementals: In magical tradition and ceremony, spirits which govern the four corners of the earth and are associated with, or reside within, the four basic elements. They are called Sylphs (the east, air), Salamanders (the south, fire), Undines (the west, water), and Gnomes (the north, earth).

EMF: stands for electro-magnetic field. EMF meters measure the intensity of the energy given off by an object. Ghost hunters believe that spirits give off EMF energy and that sudden unexplained increases in intensity may indicate the presence of an entity.

Empath: An individual who is particularly sensitive to the psychic emanations of his or her surroundings, even to a degree of telepathically receiving and experiencing the emotions of others in their proximity. Obviously, psychic empathy can be regarded as a mixed blessing, and the empath must learn to gain a measure of control over this ability.

Entity: A disembodied "consciousness" commonly referred to as ghost, spirit or (if of an apparently malicious or resentful nature) demon.

Exorcism: Ceremonial expulsion of invading spiritual/demonic entities from a person or dwelling, present in virtually every worldly culture. The Jewish and Catholic Christian faiths each have a formal 'Rite of Exorcism' to be conducted by the respective Rabbi or Priest.

Extra: A shape or a face that is said to have supernaturally appeared on film and cannot be explained away as fraud, faulty film or developing flaws.

Extra-terrestrials: Life forms originating on planets other than our own. This term usually refers to highly advanced visitors from other worlds, who journey to our sphere in space crafts with the probable intention of observing and studying our species.

Fetish: Aside from the modern sexual connotation, a fetish is a shamanistic tool in the form of a figurine, animal part or a pouch containing items with magical associations.

Floating Orb: A spherical image, usually translucent white, though sometimes of a reddish or bluish hue, which inexplicably registers on photographic film and videotape, also known as "Globule."

Frank's Box: Frank Sumption says he received instructions for building the device from disembodied entities. His first box was built in 2002, and he has made fewer than five dozen. While anyone can build one from his schematics, there seems to be something especially effective about the boxes hand-made by Sumption himself.

On line you can find information on how to construct one and people are even offering to make one for you for a small fee. Some even will charge you for asking questions or having a session for you to ask your questions of the dead who so apply want to talk to you.

So what is Frank's Box and how does it work? Is an inexpensive Ghost Box you can make and use. It is said to capture EVPs and stores your session in a .wav file for later review of sharing.

Frank's Box allows for two-way communication with the other side, in a way that is more interactive than typical EVPs. Frank's Box or the Ghost Box as it has come to be known is an electronic system, or method of sprit communication, also known as instrumental trans-communication, or ITC. Simply put Frank's Box scans AM/FM and low band frequencies to create a noise matrix from which the dead — as well as other entities — can use to modulate for messages.

Ghost: The image of a person witnessed after his/her death, reflecting the appearance of the living, physical body yet less substantial. These forms often seem to exist in a dream-like state of semi-awareness, at times though not always cognizant of their human observers. Also, a generic term used for a number of different supernatural entities.

Ghost Hunting: Various methods of investigating reports of ghosts and hauntings and determining their authenticity.

Ghost Lights: Strange balls of light, that appear in specific locations, often for an extended period of time but which have no explanation. They are thought to be of natural origin, possibly pertaining to earthquakes, fault lines, railroad tracks or water sources, but remain a mystery. Most such lights have a legend attached to them, usually involving a person who has been beheaded. The light is then explained as this person searching for their missing head.

Globule: An anomaly where-in floating, circular forms appear on photographs or videotape, which seem indicative of spirit activity. Globes are a natural containment formation of the meniscus of liquid, as in gas containing bubbles; perhaps the interaction of energy and a quasi-physical substance produced by spiritual manifestations results in a similar effect, the globules being an initial containment of energy. Presently, all we know is that they continue to appear, and extraneous possible causes such as moisture, light refraction or emulsion seepage, etc., have been considered and ruled out.

Golden-rod: A rare anomaly seen in videotape recorded at the site of a suspected haunting, appearing as bright, white or yellowish lines rapidly moving across a room.

Haunted Object: A type of haunt that involves a psychic echo or imprint on a particular object that the ghost had a particular attachment to in their physical life. Paintings, Toys, Photgraphs personal belongings, Toys etc..

Haunting: The repeated manifestation of supernatural phenomena attached to a specific locale. The activity may appear as physical apparitions, sights, sounds, smells or cold areas. Hauntings may continue for years or may only last for a brief period of time. Hauntings can be categorized into four (usually) distinct types, these being Intelligent (responsive), Poltergeist (likely initiated by pent-up stress on a subconscious level), Residual (replay) and Demonic (non-human origin).

Hex: A magical working, or "spell," cast to influence a person's will or fate, most often referring to a curse rather than a blessing or healing.

Hobgoblin: Mischievous sprite (fairy, spirit) who delights in perpetrating pranks upon hapless humans, once widely believed in and dreaded throughout Europe and Celtic regions. (Caution: It is theorized that these diminutive denizens of the netherworld will, upon occasion, interfere in psychic investigations by devices such as misplacing directions and telephone numbers, draining flashlight and camera batteries, and even pulling keys right out of investigators' pockets!) I assume that anyone who reads the proceeding caution will realize it is farcical!

Hypnosis: A state of profound mental focus, actually self-induced although an external agent - a "hypnotist" - often acts as the catalyst, or director, for the subject entering this state. Also known as "Mesmerism" after Franz Anton Mesmer who first popularized this practice (utilizing magnets as his props) during the last two decades of the 18th century. As concerns paranormal investigation, hypnosis is sometimes used as a vehicle for "past lives regression" and memory restoration in suspected (alien?) abduction cases.

Icon: A rendering or image of particular (often religious) significance.

Incubus: Stemming from medieval lore, a demonic entity capable of sexually arousing and sometimes assaulting human females. Cases of apparent incubus attacks continue to be documented, suggesting a germ of reality behind the myth.

Infestation: Repeated and persistent paranormal phenomena generally centered on a particular location or persons "Also known as a haunting."

Influence: An invisible entity of undetermined nature, affecting the inhabitants of a dwelling. This may initially manifest as an inexplicable feeling of uneasiness, then be followed by more definite signs which reveal a haunting.

Lepke: A very unique and interesting type of spiritual manifestation, a ghost which has the appearance of a solid, living person, may even converse with someone, then suddenly vanishe's. "We were talking, I turned to face her again, and she was just gone!" Such apparitions are most often reported to have been encountered within, or immediately outside of cemeteries.

Levitation: A phenomenon sometimes encountered in hauntings, particularly with Poltergeists, rare yet credibly reported, where solid objects (including persons) are moved and lifted by an unseen force. The first historically documented occurrence was that of St. Francis of Assisi in the 14th century.

Ley lines: Hypothetical alignments of a number of places of geographical interest, such as ancient monuments and megaliths. Their existence was suggested in 1921 by the amateur archaeologist Alfred Watkins, whose book

The Old Straight Track brought the alignments to the attention of the wider public.

The existence of alignments between sites is easily demonstrated. However, the causes of these alignments are disputed. There are several major areas of interpretation.

Archaeological: A new area of archaeological study, archaeogeodesy, examines geodesy as practiced in prehistoric time, and as evidenced by archaeological remains. One major aspect of modern geodesy is surveying. As interpreted by geodesy, the so-called ley lines can be the product of ancient surveying, property markings, or commonly travelled pathways. Numerous societies, ancient and modern, employ straight lines between points of use; archaeologists have documented these traditions. Modern surveying also results in placement of constructs in lines on the landscape. It is reasonable to expect human constructs and activity areas to reflect human use of lines.

Cultural: Many cultures use straight lines across the landscape. In South America, such lines often are directed towards mountain peaks; the Nazca lines are a famous example of lengthy lines made by ancient cultures. Straight lines connect ancient pyramids in Mexico; today, modern roads built on the ancient roads deviate around the huge pyramids. The Chaco culture of Northwestern New Mexico cut stairs into sandstone cliffs to facilitate keeping roads straight.

New Age: The ley lines and their intersection points are believed by some people[who?] to resonate a special psychic or mystical energy, often including elements such as geomancy, dowsing or UFOs, stating that, for instance, UFOs travel along ley lines (in the way that one might observe that cars use roads and highways). This belief postulates that points on lines have electrical or magnetic forces associated with them.

Skeptical: Skeptics of the existence of ley lines often classify them as pseudoscience. Such skeptics tend to doubt that ley lines were planned or made by ancient cultures, and argue that apparent ley lines can be readily explained without resorting to extraordinary or pseudoscientific ideas.

Lurking Enigma: "Lurk" means to furtively move about, and I can think of no more appropriate term to describe this phenomenon - a type of entity which can be visible to human observers, yet appears in distorted, unidentifiable forms. Common traits reported by witnesses include glowing red or silver eyes, dark color (fur or feathers), startling speed and agility, in some cases winged and capable of flight, as with the 'Jersey Devil.' Although such nebulous creatures seem to mean us no harm, encounters with them can be terrifying, and provoke much curiosity. As one would expect, they are extremely elusive.

Miracle: A wondrous and beneficial event apparently brought about by supernatural/divine agent.

Materialization: A ghost appearing visually, suddenly or gradually, sometimes indistinct, sometimes seemingly quite solid.

Matrixing: The natural tendency for the human mind to interpret sensory input, what is perceived visually, audibly or tactilely, as something familiar or more easily understood and accepted, in effect mentally "filling in the blanks."

Mumiai: Native American Indian spirit which behaves in the manner of a Poltergeist.

Necromancy: The practice of communicating with the dead to obtain knowledge of the future, others' secrets, etc. An archaic term, the necromancer was said to employ magic spells and conjuration to summon, then banish, the spirits of the dead.

Night Glasses or Night Vision Glasses: Are telescopes or binoculars with a large diameter objective. Large lenses can gather and concentrate light, thus intensifying light with purely optical means and enabling the user to see better in the dark than with naked eye alone. Often night glasses also have a fairly large exit pupil of 7 mm or more to let all gathered light into the user's eye. However, many people can't take advantage of this because of the limited dilation of the human pupil. To overcome this, soldiers were sometimes issued atropine eye drops to dilate pupils. Before the introduction of image intensifiers, night glasses were the only method of night vision, and thus were widely utilized, especially at sea. Second World War era night glasses usually had a lens diameter of 56 mm or more with magnification of seven or eight. Major drawbacks of night glasses are their large size and weight.

Active infrared night vision combines infrared illumination of spectral range 700nm–1000nm – just below the visible spectrum of the human eye – with CCD cameras sensitive to this light. The resulting scene, which is apparently dark to a human observer, appears as a monochrome image on a normal display device.

Because active infrared night vision systems can incorporate illuminators that produce high levels of infrared light, the resulting images are typically higher resolution than other night vision technologies. Active infrared night vision is now commonly found in commercial, residential and government security applications, where it enables effective night time imaging under low light conditions. However, since active infrared light can be detected by night vision goggles, it is generally not used in tactical military operations.

Orb: The term orb describes unexpected, typically circular artifacts in photographs. Sometimes the artifact leaves a trail, indicating motion. Orbs, in most cases turn out to be dust or some type of inscect as well.

Ouija (Board): A piece of wood bearing the letters of the alphabet that is used as a tool to make contact with the spirit world. Sitters place their fingers lightly on the planchette (or pointer) by which the spirits can spell out messages on the board. Experienced researchers vehemently advise against their usage.

Pact: The belief, prevalent in the late middle ages through the Renaissance, that someone could trade his or her soul in return for worldly gain.

Paranormal: A word meaning "unknown" or "beyond the normal" that has come to refer to events that are unexplainable.

Parapsychology: the Avenue of paranormal studies and research relating chiefly to psychic abilities (e.s.p., telepathy) and spiritual phenomena.

Pentacle/Pentagram: The traditional five-pointed star design, with its interior pentagon delineated, generally representing both spirituality and protection when point "up"; when inverted, it is said to signify diabolism.

Phantom: Another name for "ghost" or "spirit" although, interestingly, many use the word "phantom" to refer to ghosts that have been seen wearing cloaks or robes.

Phantom Lights: Sometimes they can be attributed to blue methane flame produced by swamp gas, or electrical discharges in the form of what is termed ball lightning or perhaps even misplaced fireflies. Yet, in other instances, the phenomenon of floating lights observed over water, the edge of woods, , lonely back roads and in the windows of darkened houses just can't be dismissed by ordinary explanations. These might be globules which coalesce and intensify in luminosity to the point where they become visible in dark surroundings.

Poltergeist: Literally means "noisy ghost" in German. Although it actually refers to Traditional ghosts and hauntings, in other cases, it can be used to describe the work of a human agent. In this situation, the knockings and the movement of objects is caused by an outward explosion of kinetic energy from the human mind. Most poltergeist outbreaks are short-lived.

Possession: Invasion of the human mind by a spiritual or demonic entity, where the invading agent for a span of time, influences or entirely subverts the personality of the human host. It is in these instances that the boundaries of psychology, religion and spiritualism are rendered less distinct.

Precognition: The psychic perception of future events or conditions.

Psychic: An all-encompassing word that is used to describe a person who is allegedly sensitive beyond the normal means. Such a person may be able to see and hear things that are not available to most people.

Psychic Vampire: This is a term for individuals who seem to instinctively draw and absorb the psychic energies from others, usually while conversing with (or at) them.

Psychokinesis (PK): The ability to move physical objects using only the power of the mind. In many poltergeist-like cases, human agents affect objects in an unconscious manner.

Radiant Child: The apparition of a child which is seen glowing or surrounded by a bright aura.

Rapping: Can refer to sounds that occur at a location that is experiencing a haunting or be one of the earliest forms of spirit communication in which mediums and spirits work out a code by which questions can be asked and then answered by raps from the spirits.

Reciprocal Apparition: A rare type of ghost sighting when both the spirit and the human witness see and respond to one another.

Reincarnation: The belief that a person's soul will, following bodily death, inhabit a new body in a long cycle of rebirths, purportedly for the soul's evolution through gaining experience.

Residual (Haunting): Psychic imprint of a scene which is repeatedly played out, where the witness of such phenomenon essentially is peering into the past. The ghostly participants of these time-displacements often seem unaware of their living observers.

Retro cognition: The psychic perception of past events or conditions.

Revenant: An entity which projects an appearance of being distressed or misplaced.

Sanguinor: A person exhibiting vampirism tendencies (the desire to ingest blood) and attributes. These may be either contrived or pathological.

Satan: Hebraic term for "Adversary," the "Tester" in the Biblical Book of Job, the most familiar name of the Devil, the "Fallen Angel" and the "Evil One." Investigators sometimes come across evidence of the activities of satanic cults, who perform animal sacrifices and apparently believe that desecrations and obscenities are devotions to their dark lord.

Séance: A group effort to contact the spirit world. In standardized format, the lighting of the chamber in which the séance is conducted is subdued, and the participants sit around the table, either holding hands or with hands palm down, flat against the table's surface and with fingertips touching those of the adjacent partners. A candle generally is set on the center of the table. The appointed director or "medium" addresses the spirit(s) with whom contact is sought, and then it's "We await a sign..."

Shade: An entity resembling a once-living being (human or animal).

Shaman: A tribal priest who, following much preparation and rite of initiation, uses the forces of magic to affect healings and divinations.

Silky: A female ghost which is attired in a rustling silk garment (sometimes seen, other times just heard) and performs domestic chores for a household after the occupants have retired for the night.

Specter (*or Spectre*): Another term for ghost.

Spirit: A discarnate being, or ghost, that exists in an invisible realm.

Spirit Photography: A term used for both legitimate attempts to capture ghosts and paranormal energy on film. Also, for the work of fraudulent photographers during the Spiritualist era.

Spirit Rescue: Attempting contact with entities, intended to alleviate the entities' distress and aid them in the resolution of their conflicts, and in "crossing over" to a higher, spiritual plane.

Spiritualism: A faith based on the idea that life continues after death and that communication between the living and the dead can, and does, take place.

Spunkies: The sad spirits of unnamed, unchristian or unbaptized children, believed by old Gaelic and English tradition to wander country roads in search of someone who will name them.

Succubus: "Female" counterpart of the incubus, a demonic entity said to inspire lust in men (and most inconveniently!), sometimes capable of physically attacking and inflicting injuries (bruises & slashes). Following a nocturnal visitation from a succubus, the human victim will always feel ill and depleted of vitality, and inexplicably "un-clean."

Supernatural: Events or happenings that take place in violation of the laws of nature, usually associated with ghosts and hauntings.

Synchronicity: Unexplained system of causal interaction which binds together events, actions and thought, manifesting as uncanny coincidences. Term for and existence of this phenomenon was first proposed by pioneering psycho-analyst, Carl Gustav Jung (a contemporary of Sigmund Freud). Synchronicity indicates there is more to the Universe than our understanding of simple cause and effect, and that the subtleties of the mind and matter are somehow interconnected.

Table-tipping: An experiment in psychokinesis (PK) which can fairly easily be replicated. Three or four participants lightly place their fingers along the edges of a small table top, then in unison chant "table move, table move..." With sufficient cooperation and concentration, and after several minutes of chanting, the table should start to wobble, pivot on its legs and possibly even lead the participants on a scurry about the room.

Talisman: A design or inscription that is worn, carried or displayed, for the purpose of invoking strength, power, protection or the aid of spirits.

Telekinesis: A psychic phenomenon where-in objects are remotely displaced and moved around, solely by the powers of the mind.

Teleportation: The appearance, disappearance, or movement of human bodies and physical objects through closed doors or over some amount of distance using par-anormal means. Such events often are reported to take place during hauntings.

Thought Transference: The telepathic transmitting of images and messages from the mind of one person to that of another.

Ultra-terrestrials: Beings who appear human and visit our plane of existence with some form of message or mission, then inexplicably vanish. Speculation abounds!

Vampire: A demonic (?) entity in the form of a de-ceased person, which perpetuates itself by draining the blood or psychic energy of the living.

Vortex: pl. Vortexes or Vortices. An anomaly which sometimes shows up in still photographs taken at the site of a suspected haunting, appearing as a translucent white, tube or funnel shaped mass. Some researchers believe this may be a porthole to the spirit realm.

Wraith/Wrayth: The image of a person appearing shortly before or after his or her death; term can also be applied to a ghost. Also, an apparition that is generally supposed to be an omen of death.

Zarcanor: A malevolent spirit which attacks people while they're asleep, inspiring nightmares, and sometimes even inflicting minor injuries such as scratches, bruises and what appear to be finger marks. The name is possibly of Slavic origin.

Zoomorphism: Representation of a deity or devil with animal attributes.

What Are Shadow People?

From my research, shadow people, also regarded as shadow beings, seem to center around one particular person or place , no one knows exactly why this is so. They appear as dark silhouettes that take on a human appearance. Some reports have been of seeing a hat or some type of cloak, and most turning out to be generally of male origin. They, for the most part are quite flighty... They seem to want to watch you from afar, and once they notice your onto them, take off in a flash. That's not to say they all behave that way... I know as far as my team is concerned we have notice them appearing as swirling dark smoke, and a bit mischievous at times.

On one investigation, they were down right nasty at times. With a few of the team members, "Mostly Christen" feeling a pure sense of evil, which made her sick, and had to be taken out of the house. If you happen to do a little research on the matter..."although that's why I decided to write this volume in the series, so you don't have too! Everything, you'll ever need to know about them, will be in this book lol!" But, for some reason if you should decide to do some of your own detective work, you'll find many, and I mean many...accounts of Shadow People being reported all across the world. Just in the past ten years, there have been more reports of these beings then there ever was in the decades before. But if you really dig deep you'll find all throughout history, these beings have been very much around us right from the get go!

One thing to... "Remember!" Shadow People, should never be considered ghosts! They are a whole other ball of wax... Disembodied spirits of people who have passed on, and appear to take on the appearance of the dearly departed, are what Ghosts are. Then you have your classic Orbs "which in most cases, turn out to be dust particles or insects!" Ectoplasm, along with glowing mists have also been known to be a sighting of a ghost. Shadow people on the other hand, " At least in most cases..." are not of human form and quite disturbing to say the least. And I have yet, to hear a shadow person communicate with any person or investigator out there. The only thing I have ever felt and my team as well have felt... was a deep feeling of intense fear and dread, coupled with panic and even at time a small fragment of paralysis, while being in the pretense of these dark shadow people.

Another thing I would like to add is that shadow people can be detected by all animals, and you will know it! They will start acting like there on crack and filled with hostility lol. If you have ever seen a dark matter moving extremely fast and traveling through solids in a blink of an eye, you've just seen a shadow person.

Now with all that being said... Experiencing direct visual contact is very rare! They usually are very good at disappearing, right before you can see them fully and clearly.

110

And have a habit of always being seen out of the corner of your eyes. But take special note of mirrors in a house or location you are investigating...more often then not you'll catch them in mirrors! OK, Below I have a few of proposed explanations of the shadow people phenomena:

1) One theory is that, shadow people are just manifested thought forms, from a heavy collection of negative psychic energy. This could be from and area that was involved in a traumatic event, such as a murder, suicide, or just a location where may evil people just hung out. Negative energy can create substance, and only gets stronger when it feeds on fear or negative emotions.

2) Can you say "ALIENS!" Some people out there in the paranormal world, believe that these shadow people could be some form of inter-dimensional beings. Or just another dimensional being, who for some reason or the other, has been able to overlap with our dimension, so we can see it vaguely. And that's the reason they believe when we do see one, it's usually a very misty and fleeting moment.

3) Lastly, some even believe they could very well be Guardian Angels as well. But, still that doesn't really explain, their malevolent behavior in some cases.

Now here's a more scientific explanation, of what might be going on:

1) Have you ever heard of HYPNOAGAGIA (waking sleep) what it all boils down to is a state of semi-consciousness where a person is basically half asleep and have awake " I spend most of my time that way lol!" Just kidding...but sometimes I feel like that! Anyway, the whole idea is that you can pretty much think somewhat clearly, but at the same time see images that you would while you're sleeping..."Pretty weird stuff! but, it does indeed happen." And this can be responsible for at least some of the supernatural cases, if not most by typically honest, and rational thinking people out there.

2) The good old ELECTROMAGNETIC FIELD, this one can work you over pretty well if it's strong enough! That's why it's so important to establish a good baseline before you begin any investigation. If you have a location with a real erratic or powerful electromagnetic field, "just forget it!" move onto some other location... Reason being, no matter what type of equipment you're using, it's going to be subjected to, some very strange electrical play with with your synapses of your brain. And what this does is make you really believe you are seeing and hearing ghosts, shadow people or maybe even aliens. Now where does this mostly occur? Well you can surely bet, that most of your really old buildings or homes, that are littered with substandard wiring are going to be pretty high in the electromagnetic field area. Next you have your power-plants, and of course you even have areas of the natural variety that give off strong magnetic fields.

The one thing that I find very puzzling is the fact that all these alleged eyewitnesses, report seeing shadow people wearing a hat. And till this day... they remain very difficult to explain in objective scientific terms. Oh and did I forget to mention, the shadow persons spotted wearing the hat has been reported more times by children of the age of four. "Kinda of creepy..."

Now with all that being said, I suggest... you be aware of your surroundings, get plenty of sleep! And "Most, Importantly!" Not jump to any conclusions! And just realize, that your brain is very powerful onto itself, and could at times, dig up some pretty crazy stuff from your subconscious and bring it into full view, if you go into an investigation that's filled with negative energy. But, with the proper rest before an investigation... that should, keep all the false reporting to a minimum.

The following pictures represent, a shadow being transforming...it was taken from a web cam that was connected to a laptop. Whether it's real or fake, has not been proven YET! But, surely makes for an interesting photo.

Shadow People & Sleep Paralysis

Shadow people and sleep paralysis seem to share the same episodes, or at least some of the same conditions. There have been reported by many people, who have experienced the sighting of these shadow people for themselves that seem to appear just before going to sleep and right after waking up. (Remember, Sleep Paralysis has been linked to cause hallucinations!) But, even if this were the case...that doesn't explain the fact that so many people have witnessed these beings, while fully and wide awake.

So what exactly is sleep paralysis you may ask? Sleep Paralysis is believed to be a condition that temporarily paralyzes the body minutes after waking from your sleep. Another known name for this condition is called hypnopomic paralysis. And on the opposite side of the spectrum, just before falling to sleep the scientific term hypnagogic paralysis is used to explain this condition.

It's in the same relationship that normally occurs during REM (Rapid Eye Movement) sleep.

From what I understand it's a really weird type of feeling...because even though your brain is now awake, your body is still paralyzed (unable to move) and if that wasn't bad enough... you start to see things (Hallucinate) also known as going through hypnagogic hallucinations.

But many people, who seem to be affected by this, really do believe what is happening to them... to be a dream. And this is probably the main reason, why there are so many recounting's of past dreams of people lying frozen and unable to move. (UFO Abduction cases, come to mind.) So with that being said, the hallucinatory aspect of

114

this, is that sleep paralysis makes it very hard for the person to be able to tell if what is happening is a dream or a reality.

As far as how long these episodes can last, well the jury is still out on that one. But usually anywhere from just a few seconds to roughly a few minutes, but no one really knows for sure. This must be quite frustrating for the person going through an episode. One idea that popped up, is if the person can be facing his/hers alarm clock during an episode, they may be actually very surprised at how little the time has ticked away, for an episode that may of seemed like hours have gone by.

Still to this day, very little is really known about the mechanics of sleep paralysis. However, it's been suggested by some in the field, to be linked with post-synaptic inhibition of the motor neurons that are located in the pons region of the brain. For example: Melatonin at low levels could possibly stop depolarization current from happening in the nerves, which in turn...prevents muscle stimulation.

Another substantial link to this disorder for those frequently going through these episodes is NARCOLEPSY. But, it has also been said, through countless studies that a great percentage of people throughout the world will experience sleep paralysis at least once or twice during there time here on earth. "I haven't gone through it...yet."

Down below is a list, of various factors that just may increase the chances of experiencing both paralysis & hallucinations:

1) Sleeping while facing upwards (also known as the supine position)

2) The more stress you have in your life, can bring this about.

3) Sudden changes in lifestyle or even environmental changes

4) A lucid dream that comes before the episode

Involuntary movements with your eyes closed before sleep, usually happening while imagining for long periods of time.

Types of Shadow People

Before I go ahead and list the types of shadow people that are the most common in the paranormal world. I would like to make a statement... "We as humans are people who have always been conditioned to fear the dark. It's in our nature to believe that anything, black and shadowy must be of evil origins. But, I'm here to tell you that is just not true!" Do I have any proof of that? No... But, I have witnessed many dark shadows, through my investigations, and quite frankly... Some of them I felt

116

quite comfortable with, while others I felt very much on edge, like something very bad was about to happen, if we didn't leave right now. Anyway, you don't have to be a sensitive to feel these things. After awhile of doing many investigation, you just seem to develop a sense for these things that go bump in the night. Much like a cop, who has been in law enforcement most of his life, has a sick sense to know when a situation is about to turn to the ugly. Below are the most common types you'll be most likely to run into, six to be exact... "So Far!"

1) Shadow People of Human Form

Probably the most common to be seen. They appear with such details as you may have guessed already...eyes, ears, nose...the only thing that seems to be missing from these encounters are the hands and hair. Witnesses have reported in most cases that they are of male origin. They don't seem to hang around for long, maybe at most a few seconds. They are also usually a dark semi-transparent shadow form. The feeling you get from these guys, as far as witnesses are concerned, is the feeling of being watched...not really threatening... and as soon as they are spotted they tend to flee very quickly, through objects such as doors & solid walls.

2) Shadow people of the Black Mist or Smoke Form

These shadowy beings seem to provoke more un-easiness with witnesses. They also show a very intelli-gent side to them, interacting with the witnesses and the surroundings they are in. Feelings you may get from the-se types of shadow people, are feelings of malevolence and complete dread. Much, much more than you would encounter from a human shaped shadow person, men-tioned above.

3) **The Infamous Hat Man**

Mostly seen by four year old's..." The wife and I, have a theory about this one!" We believe it's Abraham Lincoln! My wife (Teri) was actually the one who pointed this out to me. She told me, what was the one president that chil-dren of that age learned about in pre-school. It was Abraham Lincoln! And if you really think about it... To a four year old " Heck even to some of the adults out there...myself included!" He was kinda, a creepy looking fellow, Tall and lanky, his face all sunken in, wearing "You guessed it!" A tall black hat!" Now, with that being said, there's no concrete evidence of this...but, to us it sure does make sense. "Good one Hun! :)" Now, that doesn't explain all of the sighting by witnesses, who claim to see the hat of the shadow people, particularly the brim of the hat equaled to the width of their shoulders. They also seem to be very curious about the witnesses them-selves. Feeling's that have been reported from these beings, are of dread and paralysis, but not as much as, the experience you would get from the black smoke shadow person.

118

4) Animals of the Shadowy Nature

I have yet to experience one of these, and I have been doing this for quite some time! But, there are a few witnesses to this out there. In any case, they are very rare to see. Much like the human counterpart, they are seen as dark and semi-transparent creatures. The size of these creatures have been related, to the size of your average guinea pig or pet rabbit, and they to can run very quickly through walls if inside, and through fences and trees if outside.

5) The Peek-A-Boo Shadow

Witnesses have described this paranormal occurrence, as a small child size shadowy person, which loves topeek around corners and takes off in a blink of an eye when noticed. The reports on these little curious, shadow beings are of witnesses only being able to spot them out of their peripheral vision, (Out of the corner of their eyes). Like most of the shadowy figures out there, curiosity seems to be a major trait to these paranormal beings.

6) Shadow People with the Scary Red Eyes

These guys would have to be the scariest shadowy beings to ever come across and witness! Luckily for me, I haven't ever faced one of these evil creatures. "I don't think my wife would care for me bringing one of these

119

guys home with me lol!" From what I understand about these shadowy creatures, they download in the witness, extreme terror and paralysis. Many believe they are the pure embodiment of evil.

Can Shadow People Hurt You

Every now and than we get phone calls, from someone wondering if shadow people can actually hurt you?

Out of all the phenomenon's out there...I would safely say that Shadow People always seems to be the most reported by everyday people. Most of them are never really of human form, "although they may resemble slightly a human form..." but tend to be more of a very black blurred, and shifting shape that never really has a defined form. And also like I mentioned earlier, some appear with glowing red eyes, and others adoring a hat of some sort.

Some reported theories of what these beings just may be are as follows:

* Demons

* Aliens

* Inter-Dimensional entities

* Ghosts/Spirits that are having a hard time fully manifesting

* Ghosts/Spirits that just choose to represent themselves as Dark Shadowy Beings.

* Travelers from another time..."Way out there!"

* Someone traveling out of their body (Out Of Body Experience)

* A Manifestation, of someone who is highly Stressed.

* Entities that were never human to begin with.

* Or possibly even Evil Spirits.

Most claims tend to be of a threatening nature. But, the reality of it all is we are conditioned to fear what we can't see or explain with a rational mind. Granted, that some shadow people just may be malevolent, and may in fact have some sort of dark intent. But, I'm here to tell you...that what ever the case may be...it's a very, very rare if not utterly impossible for any type of shadow being to ever bring serious physical harm to you.

The team and I, feel that most sightings of Shadow People have some sort of scientific explanation to it. The biggest factor to consider is the levels of electromagnetic fields (E.M.F.) Any house or building that's really old just may have some improperly shielded or broken wire within it. Not to mention a lot of electrical devices give off an abnormally high electromagnetic field. It's been proven again and again, that the effects on the human body from receiving such high doses can, cause paranoia, nausea and even cause a small current of electricity to build up in your body. If that happens, it can cause dark spots to be seen in your vision, and cause other not so pleasant ailments to your physical body.

Yet another possible explanation could be, low frequency causing vibrations through the body. Possible culprits: Ceiling Fans, Certain types of music, Equipment rattling all these things can cause enough vibrations to rattle your eyeballs a bit, enough to cause shadows to be seen, with a number of other visual anomalies. Most of these sounds are going to be below the range that a human can hear.

And remember what I mentioned earlier... People, who seemed to go through this at night time, while they are at rest in bed, may just have a sleep disorder known as Hypnagogia, where they are right in between being a sleep and awake at the same time.

Other causes of seeing shadow people can come from Carbon Monoxide, Toxic Vapors, and the use of drugs from a legal standpoint or even from the not so legal standpoint. Again, it can also be from a mental illness. So as you can see...it is always best to rule out all the possible explanations before leaning towards the paranormal one's. By doing this you will not only, save yourself from

any undue fear...but also be able to, help your client re-
duce their fear as well.

Now with all that being said! We can never be "totally"
certain, whether shadow people do in fact exist. Although, we have had many claims, from many witnesses,.
who have been together to witness these dark shadowy
beings at the same time. And even our team, has caught
some pretty crazy looking shadow entities that have no
real logical explanation for.

As always when dealing with stuff of the paranormal nature, "Good Hard Evidence!" has always seemed to elude
us Ghost Seeking professionals. But rest assured... we
are constantly, getting better and better technology that
will in no doubt aid us all, in finally getting the much
needed and well deserved evidence to bring to the
naysayers! Our team, right now! Is running some high
tech experiments that we hope will give us some incredible images of the most elusive Shadow People.

Ghost Seeking Forms

This form is just something for you to build on. It based on the form my group uses for outdoor investigations. Feel free to change it to suit your own needs, it's just template to help get you strted

(Sample Proposal Letter to gain access to a site for an investigation)

Wednesday, April 16, 2012

To Whom It May Concern:

I represent a small group of student researchers, in the field of paranormal studies.

As part of our ongoing education, we must coordinate our research efforts on historical sites, including cemeteries, churches, parklands, etc.

We seek permission for the four of us to have access for 1 (ONE) evening, preferably this week sometime, it would be after regular gate hours, for a duration of 4 hours, from 7pm until 11pm, in order to conduct the following field investigation:

1. Photography, standard and infrared, 3 rolls (24 exposures per roll), for location verification

2. A small tape recording unit, for documentation of our efforts

3. A few other tools, such as flashlights (for obvious reasons), compass, candles for emerg. light source, and spare film, batteries and tapes, as backup, and a small hand-held electric field sensing device, as well as a notebook to record the steps as we go through them.

We expect this to be a dry run for future coordination of professional research, upon earning our certification. It will also establish base readings so that we may more ably gauge when future readings are anomalous.

Our research is dependent on clear weather, and will have to be postponed if fog, rain, high winds, snow or other inclement weather occurs on the set date and time. We will notify you of any cancellation, and if there is a need to reschedule, your permission will again be sought.

We understand, and fully respect that we will be on private property at all times, and all due consideration will be given, so that no damage come to any burial sites, mementos, or any part of your property. If through accident, or neglect on our part we do cause damage, we will repay your organization in full for the cost of repairing it.

We each have the utmost respect for all those who have a loved one buried here, and solemnly promise there will be no intoxicant consumption, horseplay, or any other disagreeable conduct, just the research as mentioned above will be done, for the duration permitted, and on the agreed site(s).

We will also notify the appropriate division of Metro Police of the date and time of our study, so that there won't be a false alarm.

We agree that we undertake this research at our own risk, and understand that your organization is not responsible for any injury or damage to the students or their instruments, while on your property.

 We agree to conduct the entire study out of view of passerby, and the general public, so as not to arouse their interest.

We ask that if you give your permission, please leave a current copy of your property's map with the caretaker, so that we can accurately make our way to our location, with no needless walking around.

Please give us your consideration, in this matter, if you require any other conditions to be met, we will accommodate them into our proposal, and sign to it. The other two students will disclose their names and contact information, and sign to your terms as well, on the date of the study. We will also provide ID, if requested.

Yours truly,

_____

Your Team Name Here (Above Line)

72 Whatever Street, City, State

Home: (xxx) xxx-xxxx   Work: (xxx) xxx-xxxx

(Sample: Release form for access to a site)

I, _____, have the authority to allow access to F,P.P.I. members and affiliated persons to _____ located in _____ for the purpose of conducting an investigation into possible paranormal occurrences or conducting field research at this location. The investigation process has been explained to me and I give F.P.P.I. permission to conduct one at this location. F.P.P.I. releases the owner of the location from any liability for injuries and/or damages incurred during the investigation. F.P.P.I. assumes responsibility for any damages to the property during the investigation.

Signed_____
Date_____

Witness_____
Date_____

(Sample: Release Form for Confidentiality and Release of Information)

F.P.P.I. respects your right to privacy. All of your personal information will be kept confidential. F.P.P.I. would like to use some or all of the information and evidence collected during the investigation for possible inclusion in our website, newsletter and other future media considerations. Please check the level of confidentiality you would like to request:

____ S.J.G.R. may not release any part of the investigation to the public.

____ F.P.P.I. may release the information providing that the identity of witnesses and clients are changed and the exact address of the location is excluded.

____ F.P.P.I. may release any/all of the information and evidence collected during the investigation.

____ Other com-ments/requests_____

_____

_____

_____

Signed_____
Date_____

Witness_____
Date_____

(Sample: Outdoor Investigation Form)

Ghost Hunt Log

Date: _____   Time: _____

Investigator: _____

Location:

_____

_____

Weath-
er:_____

_____

Other   Investigators   Pre-
sent_____

_____

_____

Equipment: Camera   Video Camera   Tape Recorder   Digital Camera

EMF   Thermometer   Night Vision

Film Speed_____   Brand_____   Exposures_____

B&W   Color   Infrared   APS

Audio Tape: Micro Cassette   Standard Cassette

length   60min   90min   120min

Video Tape: VHS   VHS-C   8mm   Digital   30min

Length   60min   90min   120min

Thermometer: Standard   Electronic   Infrared

Phenomena witnessed by investigator

Time: Phenomena:

_____

_____

_____

_____

_____

_____

_____

_____

_____

_____

_____

_____

_____

_____

_____

_____

_____

———————

——————————————————————————————

———————

——————————————————————————————

———————

——————————————————————————————

———————

——————————————————————————————

———————

——————————————————————————————

———————

Investigators initials_____

Phenomena witnessed by investigator

Time: Phenomena:

_____

_____

_____

_____

_____

Other   Com-
ments:_____

_____

_____

_____

_____

_____

_____

_____

_____

_____

____

Investigators initials:_____

Final Record

Roles of film used: _____

Audio tapes used: _____

Video tapes used: _____

Number of Psychic Photos: _____

Number of EVP recorded: _____

Phenomena captured on film: _____

Summation:

_____
_____
_____
_____

_____

_____

Investigators initials_____

(Sample: Interview Questionaire)

1. Address of site:

2. Name of witness:

3. Mailing address if different:

4. Phone number:

5. Email Address:

6. How many occupants at location:

7. How many pets:

8. Occupants' names and ages:

9. Occupants' occupations:

10. Occupants' religious beliefs:

11. Time of occupancy at the location:

12. Age of the site:

13. How many previous owners (if known):

14. History of site: (tragedies, deaths, previous complaints)

15. How many rooms in the site:

16. Has the location been blessed:

17. Has there been any recent remodeling (if so, what and where):

18. Any occupants on prescribed medication (anxiety, depression, pain, etc) Please list names and medications:

19. Any occupants using illegal drugs (this will be kept confidential):

20. Any occupants drink alcohol heavily (this will be kept confidential):

21. Any occupants interested in the occult: (Ouija, séances, psychics, spells) If so, who and what?

22. Any occupants currently seeing a psychiatrist or in therapy (this will be kept confidential): if so, who:

23. Any occupants with frequent or unexplained illnesses (if yes, describe):

24. Have any religious clergy been consulted: If so, please list church:

25. Has there been any media involvement: If so, who:

26. Have there been any other witnesses besides the occupants (names and relationships)

27. Have there been any odors: (i.e. perfumes, flowers, sulfur, ammonia, excrement, etc) If so, when, where and what:

28. Have there been any sounds: (i.e. footsteps, knocks, banging, etc) If so, when, where and what:

29. Have there been any voices: (whispering, yelling, crying, speaking) If so, when, where and what:

30. Has there been any movement of objects, If so, when, where and what:

31. Has there been any apparitions, If so, when, where and what (describe the apparition):

32. Have there been any uncommon cold or hot spots: If so, when, where and what:

33. Have there been any problems with electrical appliances: (TV, lights, kitchen appliances, doorbells) If so, when, where and what:

34. Have there been any problems with plumbing: (leaks, flooding, sinks, toilet bowls) If so, when, where and what:

35. Any occupants having nightmares or trouble sleeping: If so, who and when:

36. Have there been any physical contact: If so, who, where and what happened:

37. Are pets affected: If so, how:

38. Describe the first occurrence of the phenomena: (what and when happened?)

39. Who first witnessed the phenomena?

40. What time was the first occurrence of the phenomena?

41. What is the witness's reaction during the phenomena?

42. Were there any other witnesses during the first event?

43. How long is the average duration of the phenomena?

44. How often does the phenomenon occur?

45. Do any of the occupants feel the phenomena is threatening: If so, who and why?

46. What do the occupants believe is happening: (i.e. it's supernatural, natural, unsure, etc.):

47. Do all of the occupants agree on what is happening, Do any think it's nonsense or not happening:

48. What would you like to see accomplished from our visit?

Keep in mind that many of the people who will request an investigation will want to be comforted, educated and they may even want the spirits to leave. Whatever your approach or beliefs, be prepared for this and if you are not willing or cannot help the people in the way they would like, at least provide them with names of people who may help them. Also try to educate them so they understand what is occurring. After explaining what is happening to a witness, many will no longer be frightened or as concerned and you will have done them a great service. If you are a person or group that does offer more assistance through psychics, spirit rescues, etc. remember that the well being and the feelings of the living come first.

Para Quiz

1. What does EMF stand for?

a. Elemental Monster Forming _____

b. Electronic Machine Frequency _____

c. Electro Magnetic Field _____

d. Electronic Mine Field _____

2) What does EVP stand for?

a. Electronic Voice Panomina _____

b. Evil Violent Person _____

c. Eleven Volts Power _____

d. Elves Volunteer Program _____

3) What does it mean when a house has a residual haunting?

a. The energy of a event is caught in the material of the house and replay's it's self no matter who may be there _____

b. It's attached to someone in the house _____

c. You can never get rid of it _____

d. The entity is evil and very dangerous _____

4) What does it mean when a house has an intelligent haunt?

a. They are quite dangerous _____

b. They were never alive in the first place _____

c. When the spirt is aware of you and knows you are very aware of them they try to communicate with you _____

d. They will never cross over _____

5) Can a demon conduct a cold spot?

a. Yes _____

b. No a demon can manifest hot spots as well _____

6) Is a Ouija board safe to use for communication?

a. Absolutly not you never know who your talking to _____

b. Yes, it's a great way to get there message directly across _____

c. Only if you know how to use it _____

d. Yeah why not _____

7) What is it called if a room has high EMF all over the room?

a. a scared box _____

b. a bad place _____

c. a hot spot _____

d. a fear cage _____

8) What are some things high EMF can cause?

a. Skin irritation, nausia, hullcinations, feeling of being watched _____

b. Nose bleeds _____

c. Headachs _____

d. Bad dreams _____

9) Is it smart to provoke a spirit?

a. It's never a good idea _____

b. Depending on the spirit _____

c. If being repectful doesn't work first _____

d. Only if they are known to be mean _____

10) Why can't the human ear sometimes not hear a spirit voice

a. They have nothing to say _____

b. If you can't hear it they don't want to talk _____

c. Because there fake _____

d. Because it's just under the threshold of hertz the human ear can hear _____

11. What types of things have been reported being seen in a ghostly form?

a. Humans _____

b. Animals _____

c. Cars _____

d. All of the above _____

12. What is the technical name for experts who study ghosts?

a. Psychologists _____

b. Philosophers _____

c. Parapsychologists _____

d. Ghost hunters _____

13. What do some scientific researchers think ghosts are made up of?

a. Psychic energy

b. Dust

c. Light reflections

d. Clouds

14. Western ghost experts agree that most ghosts are not made up of solid matter.

a. True _____

b. False _____

15. What is the term for when a ghost controls the mind of a human?

a. Psycho overtake _____

b. Poltergeist _____

c. Spirit guide _____

d. Ppiritual possession _____

16. Why was Anne Boleyn beheaded?

a. She slept with her brother _____

b. She married while king henry was still married _____

c. They didn't like her _____

d. She was a sister to the first wife to henry the viii but still married _____

17. What type of ghost is commonly believed to be an evil spirit but is mostly peaceful and is known to be seen in many places throughout England?

a. Shadow _____

b. Poltergeist _____

c. Apparition _____

18. What is said to be an acid to Ghost?

a. Salt _____

b. Flashlights _____

c. Water _____

d. Dirt _____

19. Where (to official knowledege) in the amityville house has a ghost child been captured on camera?

a. On the stairs _____

b. In the hallway _____

c. Iin the former Childs bedroom _____

d. All of the above _____

20. Where do ghosts live?

a. In my house _____

b. I dont care _____

c. Every where _____

d. In grave yards _____

21. Can a ghost show up on camera?

a. Yes _____

b. No _____

c. I dont know _____

d. Only sometimes _____

22. What kind of ghost throws objects around ,closes doors, and does other physical affects?

a. Apparition _____

b. Poltergeist _____

c. Shadow _____

d. Orb _____

Ghost Seeking Resources

Ghost hunting Software

http://www.simplyghost.com/

Ghost Hunting Equipment (On a shoestring Budget)

Ebay.com

Paranormal News

http://www.paranormalnews.com/

Ghost Hunting Equipment Tutorials

Youtube.com

Free Evp Software

Audacity - I totally recommend this software, by far the best "FREE EVP" Software you can get right now. (Just GOOGLE "Audacity")

Audio Spectrum Analyzer - Killer spectrum audio software! Allowing user to analyze, the sounds you pick-up through spectrums.

EVP Assistant v1.0 Noise Generator - Mark Andrew Turner came up with this one! He's part of the EVP Research Association in the UK. To call this typical software is an understatement The only EVP software "That I know of" That can generate "White Noise" to help you catch some elusive EVP's.

AoA Audio Extractor Basic – This software extracts Audio from the background. "Pretty Cool!"

Wavosaur Audio Editor - Yet Another "FREE" EVP editor. Pretty powerful to boot!

Gimp- Free software to help you design Flyers, Logos, Edit photo's "Awesome Stuff!!!" And the best part it is free!

http://www.gimp.org/

Logo Creator V5- Another "Free" software that can be found online just do a quick "Google Search!" This program is excellent for creating your own custom Team Logo's. "I can't believe this software is free!"

Visit me online: At http://frankpotterstone.blogspot.com/ for the latest updates on new books, resources, ghost hunting tips, quizzes, photos, stories, and much more...

Para Quiz "Answers"

(Answers for pages 146-153)

1. What does EMF stand for

Correct Answer: Electro Magnetic Feild

2. What does EVP stand for

Correct Answer: Electronic Voice Panomina

3. What does it mean when a house has a residual haunt

Correct Answer: The energy of a event is caught in the material of the house and replays it's self "Over and over" no matter who's there

4. What does it mean when a house has an intelligent haunt

Correct Answer: When the spirt is aware of you and know your aware of them they try to communicate with you

5. Can a demon only conduct a cold spot?

Correct Answer: No a demon can conduct hot spots as well

6. Is a Ouija board safe to use for communication?

Correct Answer: Absolutely not you never know who you may be talking too

7. What is it called if a room has high EMF all over the room?

Correct Answer: a fear cage

8. What are some things high EMF can cause?

Correct:Answer: Skin,iratation,nausia, hullcinations,feeling of being watched

9. Is it smart to provoke a spirit?

Correct Answer: Depending on the spirit

10. Why can't the human ear, sometimes not hear a spirit voice?

Correct Answer: because it's just under the threshold of hertz the human ear can hear

11. What types of things have been reported being seen in a ghostly form?

Correct Answer: all of the above

12. What is the technical name for experts who study ghosts?

Correct Answer: parapsychologists

13. What do some scientific researchers think ghosts are made up of?

Correct Answer: psychic energy

14. Western ghost experts agree that most ghosts are not made up of solid matter.

Correct Answer: True

15. What are the terms for when a ghost controls the mind of a human?

Correct Answer: spiritual possession

16. Why was Anne Boleyn beheaded?

Correct Answer: she slept with her brother

17. What type of ghost is commonly believed to be a evil spirit but is mostly peaceful and is known to be seen in many places throughout England?

Correct Answer: Shadow

18. What is said to be an acid to Ghost?

Correct Answer: salt

19. Where (to official knowleddge) in the amityville house has a ghost child been captured on camera

Correct Answer: on the stairs

20. Where do ghosts live?

Correct Answer: every where

21. Can a ghost show up on cramra?

Correct Answer: only sometimes

22. What kind of ghost throws objects around ,closes doors, and does other physical affects?

Correct Answer: poltergeist

Wrap Up

Having read How to Ghost Hunt... you now have the knowledge you need to take with you, and be very successful on all your future Ghost Seeking Adventures with your team.

I hope this book, stays with you on all your future investigations. If you have any question, feel free to email me anytime at fpotterstone@gmail.com

Good luck!